WHAT'S
GOOD
ABOUT
GOD
?

Hoover Rupert

WHAT'S
GOOD
ABOUT
GOD
?

ABINGDON PRESS
Nashville & New York

WHAT'S GOOD ABOUT GOD?

ISBN 0-687-44870-0

Library of Congress Catalog Card Number: 70-124749

SET UP, PRINTED, AND BOUND BY THE
PARTHENON PRESS, AT NASHVILLE,
TENNESSEE, UNITED STATES OF AMERICA

In Memoriam
The Rev. Lynn Hoover Rupert, Sr.

who devoted
half a century to helping persons
know how God meets their needs

Preface

One of the most poignant phrases to come out of World War II was found in the diary of a young soldier after he had been killed in action. *Life* magazine reprinted a page from that diary which reads like this: "This is a time for a new revelation. People don't think much about religion nowadays, but we need a voice from on high, brother, and I don't mean maybe!—This thing has got out of human ability to run. I'm no religious fanatic, but we're in a situation where something better than human brains has got to give us advice."

The ensuing quarter of a century has pointed up the truth of his words. Yet man has failed to grasp the "something better" by way of advice. I happen to belong to that group of citizenry who still maintain a belief in God as the creative and sustaining power in the universe—and in human life. As a pastor I can report scores of experiences of persons within my congregation whose needs have wandered in search of solution until one day they learned how God meets those needs. I write not of an irrational belief in a religion composed of half superstition and half blind faith. I write of persons whose modest doctrinal understanding of the Christian faith brought rhyme and reason into experiences that tested their strength as well as their spirit. This is never easy because there are so many factors in our society that move against our faith in God and his power to meet our needs.

There is the open opposition of the atheist and the agnostic. I read somewhere recently that Charles Smith, president of the American Association for the Advancement of Atheism, was quoted as saying, "To tell the truth, we aren't very active any more." My observation would be that somewhere along the line that activity has been resumed with widespread vigor. Fifteen years ago a group of students at Cambridge University in England organized what they called The Cambridge Humanist Society. The Society's premise is "that human problems can, and must be faced in terms of human intellectual and moral resources without invoking supernatural authority." That pretty well forces man into a "bootstrap religion" at best. Moreover, Professor Julian Huxley found many followers in our land when he predicted that "it will be as impossible for an intelligent, educated man or woman to believe in God, as it is now to believe that the earth is flat, or that disease is a divine punishment."

More to the point of our purpose in this volume is the prevalence of patently false concepts of the nature of God and the way he works in the world. As reported in an issue of *The Christian Century,* an Australian professor of biology, Charles Birch, sees the chief enemy of Christianity today as being not communism or atheism or secularism, but that form of the Christian religion which would preserve conceptions of God that the world has already seen through as false.

Any one who works with youth today will report that youth is tired of the old cliches or religion in general. They meet many adults who have gone no further than a childish version of Christianity. These are persons in middle age who still maintain a kindergarten concept of God. Thus youth are turned off a religious quest which appears to promise little more than meaningless nonsense.

Part of the problem is a language barrier. Few youth read books of theology in great numbers because such books are seldom written with the idea that the man in the pew, let alone the kid on the street, can really understand what's being said. A seminary student in California is credited with doing a "theologian's rewrite" of Peter's Great Confession as follows: "And Jesus said to them, 'Who do you say that I am?' And they replied, 'You are the eschatological manifestation of the ground of our being; the kerygma manifested in conflict and decision in the humanized process.' And Jesus said, 'WHAT?'" And so say we when theological realities are buried in the obscurity of erudite phrases and obtuse concepts.

The journeyman preacher, faced with the perpetual shadow of next Sunday's pulpit demands, can testify that it is no simple task to seek to lead a congregation into a greater understanding of God and how he meets human needs. Now and then the pulpiteer may get by with a philosophical dissertation or a verbal theological treatise that has meaning only for the theologically oriented persons of training and background. But try that every other Sunday and sooner than he imagines the bishop, with urgent prompting from a pastoral relations committee, will provide him with a new "opportunity." To put the cookies on the lower shelf does not reduce their quality nor their tastiness. To translate theological jargon into everyday language is not necessarily to reduce irreverently the size of the God to whose love and power the preacher bears his personal witness. Rather, it is to open new windows of light on areas of thought which may have been covered up with polysyllabic dust. To Paul's question "How shall they hear without a preacher?", one may appropriately add, "And how shall they understand if he fails to speak their language?"

All of which brings us to the reason for this book being written. Certainly not because I am a professional theologian, nor because I have anything new to add to the plethora of such volumes now gathering dust on library shelves. This book is no effort to make a systematic analysis of our Christian doctrine. I may well be like the minister Kenneth Patton tells about who criticized humanism and blamed most of the ills of the world on the atheists. A humanistic philosopher friend of the pastor took issue with him. At one point he said to the clergyman, "Al, when you stand in the pulpit on Sunday and use the word 'God,' do you really know what you mean?" After some hesitation, the preacher admitted, "Well, I may not know exactly what I mean by 'God,' but the people do." I hope I do not seem dogmatic in what follows, though I claim a real element of honest certainty in my confession of faith.

Each Lenten season I use the Sunday morning sermons to preach on matters specifically related to Christian doctrine. I find people are far more anxious to hear serious considerations of Christian faith than they were when I began my ministry thirty years ago. These chapters seek in the written word to do what I try to do in the spoken word—examine some of our traditional doctrines in the light of twentieth-century science and technology and the demands upon the seeking

Christian in such a world as this, all in the richness of biblical faith and Christian tradition. I have used the resources of theologians and other writers to express formally some of the items of faith. But, I have also tried to relate those concepts to the stuff of daily living in illustrations and experiences in the process of applying these ideas to the pattern of daily life—my own and other persons.

If you are looking for a formal and systematic presentation of Christian beliefs, look eleswhere than these pages. The reference notes will provide a bibliography for that search. Once before I tried to set down in writing something of such a formal approach in a little volume entitled *What Methodists Believe*. My minister-father, upon reading the manuscript before publication, half facetiously suggested a change in title to *What One Preacher Thinks Methodists Believe*. Such modesty needs to be encouraged, I am sure, in this effort as well as that!

No author stands alone. My indebtedness is impossible of repayment. To college teachers Homer Kingsley Ebright, James S. Chubb, and Benjamin A. Gessner, to seminary professors William J. Lowstuter, Edgar A. Brightman, Albert C. Knudson, Francis Gerald Ensley, and Edwin Prince Booth, I am grateful for helping me see the necessity for every man building his own theology with emphasis on rational understanding along with the data of human experience. They cannot be held responsible for my beliefs, but to them I owe much in the developing of those beliefs. The book is dedicated to my father because he was for me the first to emphasize this process in arriving at a personal credo. He never made the mistake of dogmatic demand in Christian belief, but he never backed off from my challenge to defend his own beliefs. Thus, he helped me greatly in the fashioning of my own Christian convictions, some of which, to be sure, he, himself, could not accept.

So, I invite you to a quest for your own theology, a pilgrimage of ideas and experiences that hopefully may help you in learning for yourself how God meets your needs. This book is not a finished product from which you can lift a theology for your life. It could be a means through which you rethink your own outlook as a Christian and come to some firmer foundations for your own faith. That, frankly, is the most I would hope for as we exchange ideas through the pages that follow.

HOOVER RUPERT

Epworth Heights
Ludington, Michigan

Contents

God Enters—Incarnation

The deeper meaning of the Christian faith will escape you unless you can believe in miracles. Now, don't try to tell me you don't believe in miracles! What do you mean you don't believe in miracles—you *are* a miracle. Your parents looked down in your crib and were intrigued as are all parents with the intricate detail with which the Creator endowed your body. They couldn't examine your little finger and its functioning without an awareness of the miraculous process of creation which attached that hand to your body and gave it purpose and function. They watched you grow—all of a sudden you seemed to be as tall as your mother and you were able to discuss world affairs and sex and even religion with your father on his level. And sometimes you were beyond him. The miracle of growth was being daily illustrated in your life.

What of the mystery of love? Do you explain it simply by the chemistry of the human organism and its attracting qualities to chemical combinations in another of the same species but of a different sex? What of the mystery of death? Do you explain it simply as dust to dust and ashes to ashes? And in between the miracle of birth and the mystery of death how do you account for that which separates you from the rest of the animal kingdom who are birthed and who die? You can think and plan in a purposeful way—so can the squirrels and the ants. But you have ideals that you can make into realities in our life and environment. You have a conscience that keeps clearly before you the moral choices which you alone among the species have sensitivity enough to recognize. Yes, don't tell me you don't *believe* in miracles. You *are* a miracle.

In spite of what succeeding generations have done to it, the little town of Bethlehem is a sacred spot to the visiting Christian. I was shocked by the enormous, very old, very dark, and very depressing church which was erected a dozen or more centuries ago by Helena, the mother of Constantine. It stands over the spot where once stood the inn of Bethlehem. Actually the stable was one of a series of caves in the hillside beneath the inn. It was not uncommon for people and animals of the field to gather there for protection at night against the chill winds and winter cold.

On the spot where the manger stood there is today a golden star, worn smooth and shiny by the touch of millions of pilgrim hands. Above it is an eternal light. I can understand

16

how it was that a minister-friend reports about a hard-bitten friend of his who was present with him at this place when their group burst into singing "O Little Town of Bethlehem." As the group turned to mount the steps out of that grotto back into the chancel of the church above, this man stayed behind, and pointing to that golden star he said to my friend, "How wonderful that Jesus Christ was born. How wonderful for me that He was born. I cannot imagine what my life would have been without him." Well, can anyone? Does anyone really want to try?

The Christian faith interprets this action of God sending his emissary to earth with a doctrine called "Incarnation." God sent his son to earth as man with men to dwell—that man might know what God is like and what he expects of his children. There was an element of risk in this idea, as Robert Frost suggested:

> Pulpiteers will censure
> Our instinctive venture
> Into what they call
> The material
> When we took that fall
> From the apple tree.
> But God's own descent
> Into flesh was meant
> As a demonstration
> That the supreme merit
> Lay in risking spirit
> In substantiation.[1]

[1] From "Kitty Hawk" from *The Poetry of Robert Frost* edited by Edward Connery Latham. Copyright © 1956, 1962 by Robert Frost. Reprinted by permission of Holt, Rinehart and Winston, Inc.

Here was God's final effort to get through the density of man's mind and spirit with the divinity which is involved with humanity.

God with Us

Shortly after the close of World War II, I heard Martin Niemoeller tell of his experience in Dachau prison on Christmas Day, 1944. You will recall he was imprisoned by Hitler because of his continuing courageous declaration of the Christian faith in face of demands that he tone it down. On this day he was permitted to hold services for some of the prisoners. Few of them were to emerge alive from their imprisonment; many of them had been and would be tortured by their captors. What does a Christian clergyman say in a situation like that? Niemoeller preached on the text, "And his name shall be called Emmanuel, which means God with us." And he pointed out that they were not alone in their days of suffering and imprisonment. God was with them, even there, to save them from their sins, to comfort and strengthen them in persecution, to give them courage in the face of torture, and to keep their hope alive. They could be certain about this, he said, because in Jesus Christ, God is with us.

Consensus has it that the greatest voice in the American pulpit in the nineteenth century was that of Phillips Brooks. He can help us get our teeth into this doctrine with his simple analysis of what this doctrine is all about. The Incarnation, he said, is a doctrine about Jesus Christ, that in him humanity and divinity are united, that "God was in Christ reconciling the world unto himself." Here is doctrine about God stating that he is Christ-like, that to look at Christ is to see God, that to know Christ is to know God. Here is doctrine about man which sees the universal principle of divinity that says the man who knows Christ has lighted the spark of divinity in the human heart and is on the way toward perfecting the divine-human combination for his own life, similar to that which is perfectly combined in Jesus.

I suppose part of our problem is the fact that we celebrate Christmas many times and miss out on its deeper meaning. We get bogged down in the tinsel and trappings and miss the essential Christian doctrine involved. Or, we spend all our adoration on the baby in the manger. I well recall the mixture of humor and consternation with which a young father reported to me a question from his four-year-old youngster. Without introduction one day she inquired of him: "Why doesn't the Baby Jesus ever grow up?" She had it pretty straight, he said, that Christmas is the time for celebrating the birthday of Jesus. But she couldn't figure out why each successive year the pictures showed him only as a baby in a cradle or in his mother's arms. After all, the other birthday parties to which she had gone represented another year of physical growth for the celebrant.

That young lady put her finger on precisely one of our doctrinal problems in this area. You can expect such a question from a four-year-old, but how about adults who never get Jesus out of the cradle, but leave him eternally in the nursery

19

division? For them he never grows to the stature of the God-Man. They miss out on the real genius of the Incarnation—the human trek through infancy and childhood and adolescence into adulthood as Jesus lived it. No wonder for some he remains only "Gentle Jesus meek and mild, smile upon us, Holy Child." That pretty well shortchanges the real Christmas story—God with us, as man with man to dwell.

Miracle of God's Power

Now, don't get me wrong! I do not mean to imply that there is a simple doctrine, easily accepted and quickly understood. But, before we can go further into building our own system of Christian doctrine, we must realize how it is that God has entered human life. The Christian faith, in all its branches of denominations and schools of interpretation, is founded on the belief that God has indeed invaded human history in Jesus Christ, that in this Jesus man finds divinity and humanity united in a unique way. Jesus is the embodiment in human form of God, the Father Almighty. We can gain help from several writers who have interpreted what the Incarnation means to us.

Take St. Athanasius who lived in the early part of the fourth century A.D. He was writing about the dehumanizing of mankind which was taking place when God sent Jesus into the world. "What else could He possibly do, being God, but renew His Image in mankind, so that through it men might once more come to know Him? And how could this be done save by the coming of the very Image Himself, our Saviour Jesus Christ? . . . The Word of God came in His own Person, because it was He alone, the Image of the Father, who could recreate man made after the Image."

Bishop Gerald Ensley wrote in an article for *Religion in Life* that the Incarnation is, first of all, a doctrine about Jesus Christ, that in him divinity and humanity were united . . . And, secondly by implication, it is a doctrine about God: that he is Christlike. He is a personal being, for only such can explain the intelligence, conscience, sense of duty and God-consciousness that dwelt in Jesus."

Leslie Weatherhead adds a facet to this thought when he wrote in *Over His Own Signature,* "By that incarnation I mean that God was in Christ to a maximum fullness consonant with humanity, that God dwelt in Christ as fully as God can dwell in man without disrupting and destroying his real humanity. Christ thus was not omniscient or omnipresent or omnipotent, but at the same time he revealed the essential nature of God as fully as human nature can reveal it. In any case, deity is more importantly revealed in terms of love than in terms of power, or knowledge or omnipresence."

In language which carries some of the current theological and ecclesiastical idiom, Ross Snyder speaks of a contemporary Incarnation in *Young People and Their Culture,* "Christ is God *engaged* with the burgeoning intentions of man come of age, struggling with man's imperfections, guilts, profanations, ambiguous historymaking. He is God in *situation*—not building a perfect world, but transforming what happens into new possibility. He is not dead, nor has he left the world to its own devices."

Here we are dealing with a crucial step in Christian belief: Can you accept the doctrine of the Incarnation? Can you believe that God has come to us in Jesus Christ? Can you believe that God can come alive in any possessor of human personality, that there is something of God in every man? This, you see, is the greatest miracle of all. Why try to determine whether or not Jesus turned water into wine, fed a multitude, healed a leper, gave sight to the blind, or raised Lazarus from the grave? The basic miracle is right here—the Incarnation. It is the keystone of Christian doctrine. It is the cornerstone of Christian faith.

In terms of your own theology, you must come to grips with the Incarnation before you go further in your efforts to build your own set of ordered beliefs. Georgia Harkness made an interesting comment about this in *The Faith by Which the Church Lives:* "Apart from the Incarnation we cannot fruitfully consider the Atonement, the forgiveness of sins, regeneration through the grace of God in Christ, justification by faith, or any of the other great concepts in Paul's theology. Accept the fact that God became flesh in a good Jew who was more than a Jew, in a teacher of a new way who was more than a teacher, in a God-man who died in love and rose in triumph, in an abiding Christ who is still our Divine Companion, and these terms take on meaning. Start from the terms themselves, and they are barren abstractions. God saves us in divine mercy when we do not merit salvation, God forgives our sins, God empowers us to newness of life and to service in his Kingdom—and we know that God does this because we know Jesus as Lord."

Chances are that if you have slipped over your depth in your efforts to understand the Incarnation as a theological doctrine, you will find an expression of your own experience in Harry Webb Farrington's verses, "I Know Not How That Bethlehem's Babe," which are sung in churches every Advent:

> I know not how that Bethlehem's babe
> Could in the Godhead be;
> I only know the manger child
> Has brought God's life to me.
>
> I know not how that Calvary's cross
> A world from sin could free;
> I only know its matchless love
> Has brought God's love to me.
>
> I know not how that Joseph's tomb
> Could solve death's mystery;
> I only know a living Christ,
> Our immortality.

With Man to Dwell

In one of his books H. G. Wells tells the story of a man of affairs whose mind was so tensed and whose nerves so taut that he was in danger of a complete emotional collapse. His doctor told him that the only thing that could save him was to find "the peace that fellowship with God can give." The

23

man exclaimed, "What? To think of that, up there, having fellowship with me! I would as soon think of cooling my throat with the milky way or shaking hands with the stars."

Most of us know exactly what he meant. To keep Jesus in the manger is one thing, but to keep God "out there" somewhere is to deny life the possibility of God's love as a realized experience in the human heart. It is only when we realize that God the Creative Genius is the God who is the God and Father of our Lord Jesus Christ, that there comes into our lives that sense of divine-human encounter which the Christian faith calls personal fellowship with God in Christ. And here again we confront the miracle of the Incarnation.

The Incarnation is the miracle of God's power. For one thing, it is the miracle of *idea become incarnate*. Dr. Harry Emerson Fosdick tells us that it is only when an idea becomes incarnate that it really becomes powerful. For example, we do not fall in love with the idea of unselfishness any more than we fall in love with a geometric theorem. We fall in love with an unselfish person. And there is a difference. He goes on to say in *What Is Vital in Religion* "nobody understands human nature until he sees that at the heart of us we are photographic plates taking pictures of people. We may think we argue ourselves into righteousness. We do not. Intellect and Will are very import, but in this regard they are not primary; they are secondary. Primarily, we are photographic plates taking pictures of people."

You can illustrate this in positive and negative ways. Somebody incarnates sin until it becomes irresistibly alluring to us—that does the business. On the other hand, somebody incarnates goodness until it becomes fascinating to us and we are transformed by it, through its incarnation. Well, the idea of God becomes incarnate when we take Christ's picture on the photographic plates of our souls. The idea of God's love, his goodness, his mercy, his power—these all come alive for us when they are embodied in the Man Jesus—idea become incarnate. That's a miracle!

Here also is the miracle of *principle made reality*. So, we can establish through law and logic that love is better than hatred, that goodwill is better than hostility. But when does it become for us the real "gut-experience" the theologians write about? When we see it incarnated. Principle expressed in person makes it a reality for us. Prior to this it is but an elusive thought or an accepted logic. But when we see it come alive in a man named Jesus, the Christian principle takes on a powerful reality from which we cannot, nor do we wish to, escape.

Finally, here is the miracle of *ideal impersonated*. By that I mean an idea that is made real for us through its becoming impersonated—made real in a person. The ideal of sacrifice is accepted as essential to friendship—"Greater love has no man than that he lay down his life for his friend." But what gives body and strength to that ideal? To see it happen! To know that it happened for me. To realize I am here because someone else sacrificed his life to save mine. And in essence that is what the Christian faith is all about. That's what Christmas comes to remind us. Here is the miracle of God's power brought alive in Jesus. As Fosdick says it, "Our religion is impersonated—Christianity is Christ. And to know him and love him until his spirit is reproduced in us and the Christ of history becomes the Christ of experience—that is vital Christianity."

Clue to Reality

How do you find out what's real and what isn't? Do you succumb to the mistake of identifying the tangible with the real, and assuming that reality is only that which you can sense with one of the five physical senses? That fouls you up because one day you did discover a reality which had significance and meaning for your life. Yet this is not a tangible reality. It is in the area of what we call spiritual values. You discover what love means and you cannot make a scientific analysis of that.

Now commendably, science is dedicated to following out every clue that will give man further understanding of the nature of reality. We are deeply in the debt of our friends in the sciences who spend long months and years and lifetimes in research, which helps us know more of the world of physical reality than we could have known without them. But, demonstrable evidence in the scientific method stops short of some of the realities of life. Some it cannot measure. It cannot force them into the test tube or under the microscope. And yet, there are persons who claim that these are as real as the toothache they cannot see or the heart-anguish they feel when families are separated by distance or divorce, or the guilt feelings that linger because of real or imagined sins. And what about the positive sides of those experiential coins—

love and beauty and goodness. What clue can science give to these realities of human experience? Very little really.

Christmas comes annually to remind us that the real clue to ultimate reality is to be found in the birth of Jesus as the birth of divine truth God wanted to convey to his people. It was Plato who said, long before the time of Jesus, that the human mind is not big enough to comprehend the vast idea of God. God must have seen this clearly also. For he came to man in human form that man might have a clue to the ultimate reality of life and the world in a dimension which could be to his understanding.

Perhaps the best illustration of this is one which Sam Shoemaker used to use. He suggested that God looked down from heaven and saw men messing up everything. So he called Jesus and said, "I want you to go down to earth and help these people straighten things out. They are confused, mixed-up, and having a terrible time. They need guidance." Then he used this analogy: God is like a Father who gives an erector set or some other kind of mechanical toy to his son. It is under the tree on Christmas morning. The boy excitedly reads the directions, but he cannot make head nor tail of them. So the father gets down on the floor and helps his son. Said Sam Shoemaker, "Man had his directions, but he was all mixed up about them. So in Jesus Christ God got down from heaven onto the floor of the world and showed his children how to get the knack of living." He was giving us an additional clue—a living insight into what is ultimately worthy, of what is the ultimate reality in this world of ours.

In Jesus Christ, God came down to help us read the directions for building our lives in such a way that they are meaningful in their living and related to ultimate reality. This happened when God came to us in Christ. In fact, here was the missing crucial piece from the puzzle of life which never seemed to get worked out right before. Now the final piece is inserted and we see what the thing is all about. And that happened because of the Incarnation, because of God coming here to us and sharing our life through Jesus. And we call Jesus Emmanuel because through him we know God is with us.

Self-disclosure of the Eternal

One of the most cherished of our personal possessions is our privacy as a person. I don't care how gregarious you are, how essential it is for you to have people around all the time to keep you from getting lonely and/or bored, there are those times and experiences in your life when you want to be alone. Our form of living in houses close together, apartments wall to wall, would certainly crowd Daniel Boone out of his grave. But even so, there are times and experiences when we want to be, and make every effort necessary to be, all alone. In the days when I was a traveling national board staff member, I clocked more than a half million miles in five years. It was before commercial flying had come into its own. I learned why so many persons demand a single room in hotels during conventions and conferences, rather than to room with either a friend or a stranger. It is the need for some place to go to escape from the crowd and secure some respite in privacy. I share that demand even now (except when my wife accompanies me on such a trip, I hasten quickly and firmly to add).

I think the Incarnation reminds us that God, having failed in his efforts to reach man with disclosures of himself and his love through the world of nature, through the call of the prophets, and through the word of scripture, now gave up his divine privacy, as it were. He came into the world as a person that we might know him personally as our Heavenly Father and that we might know him through Jesus Christ and his revelation. Here is self-disclosure of the Eternal that we might know that God is with us.

Listen to the way George Buttrick puts it in *The Christian Fact and Modern Doubt*: "The disclosure of the Eternal which we covet is more than that given through the ambiguous mask of nature or vaguely through the mixed good and evil of mankind at large. The assurance cannot be through letters on a sky: we would say our eyes deceived us; nor through thundered precepts: we would say our hearts had mocked us. But a Life lived among men and rooted in our history, lived in a manner so deathless that it takes life anew in every life —that, in silence, with no violation of man's freedom, might be the revealing of the Mystery behind the flux of time. 'Now Jesus was born in Bethlehem of Judea!' "

We come to knowledge of God through a divine life lived among humankind and rooted in our human history. It is a miraculous clue to reality, a key to the self-disclosure of the Eternal. But it comes alive *to* us only as he comes alive *in* us. Only when we accept for ourselves the revelation of God in Christ can we come to know what God is really like.

29

Olin Stockwell spent three years in Red China in prison because his missionary work as a Methodist-American worker brought him into ill favor with the Communist leadership. In his book *With God in Red China,* he tells of a letter from a Chinese pastor in a northwestern village which, of course, was under Communist domination. In the letter he wrote that they no longer sang Christian hymns. They no longer attended Christian services at the church. He no longer preached the Christian message. And so on he wrote, sentences that enabled the letter to get by the Red censors. But his closing salutation also got by the censors. Just before signing his name, this Chinese pastor wrote one word: Immanuel! This beleaguered Christian pastor was expressing in one word the fact that his faith and that of the Christians under his leadership was still vitally alive even in the midst of the communist oppression. Even under the threat of red terror he bore his testimony, "God with us."

So, you still don't believe in miracles? So you cannot really celebrate Christmas as a Christian? Then there is not much point in reading further these essays in doctrine. If you stumble here, you will fall flat on your face there. For here is the keystone in the arch of your belief as a Christian, here is the cornerstone of any creed you may author to express your faith: "Immanuel—God is with us." And with that Christmas gift from God come the light and the peace and the love without which no life can be lived with effectiveness in times of darkness and war and hatred. Laurence Housman put it so well when he penned these words:

Light looked down and beheld Darkness.
"Thither will I go," said Light.
Peace looked down and beheld War.
"Thither will I go," said Peace.
Love looked down and beheld Hatred.
"Thither will I go," said Love.
So came Light and shone.
So came Peace and gave rest.
So came Love and brought Life.[2]

"And the Word was made flesh and dwelt among them."

[2] "Light Looked Down and Beheld Darkness." Reprinted by permission of the Executors of the Laurence Housman Estate.

God Lives—Certainty

In the summer of 1969, the sports world seemed to have an uncommon series of retirements of its stars. In gloomy and tearful press conferences, aging young men announced they must give up their jobs because of health and age and an apparent impossibility to keep up with the demands of the sport. One of these was Don Drysdale, one of the great baseball pitchers of our time. He added a third item to the things that traditionally are certain. For generations man has said that two things are certain: death and taxes. Now thirty-three-year-old Drysdale adds a third: for a professional athlete it is retirement. Though one looks and wonders at pitcher Hoyt Wilhelm who, at forty-six is still actively engaged in fooling major league batters with his knuckle ball.

Is that all we can say is certain? Can we add nothing to the trinity of death, taxes, and retirement? Well, sometimes we recoil from persons who are so sure of themselves. Here was a man who bought a bass violin. He took it home, drew the bow across the strings, and liked the sound very much. He kept sawing away on that one note. The next day it was the same, and the next and the next. Finally, his wife could stand it no longer. Diplomatically she said to him, "My dear, I have noticed that other people move their fingers up and down on the strings and get different notes. Why don't you try that?" The man shook his head and replied, "No, ma'am. Those people are still looking for the right note. I have found it!" And who wouldn't shrink from that kind of misguided certainty?

Arthur Koestler wrote a novel he called "The Age of Longing." In it a sophisticated American girl falls in love with a Communist. She cannot stomach his politics, she despises his philosophy of life, and she reacts to his untutored manners. But he casts a spell over her with his amazing certainty. In the face of life's baffling questions she is confused and bewildered. In contrast to this, though he is a person of no morality, he has one goal in life. He moves toward it with every muscle. It never occurs to him that he might be wrong, that his beliefs might be called into question. Such certainty carries a hypnotic quality when it confronts persons who are not anchored to any basic convictions. And we may well admire his certainty, indeed may envy it, without accepting his ideas and way of life.

The central certainty of the Christian faith is that the God of Jesus is not dead. That is, if we believe what Jesus had to

say about God. One will search his words in vain to find uncertainty in Jesus at this point.

In 1966, we were confronted with a widely publicized
theological fad which held that God is dead. Its major prophet
was Professor Thomas Altizer of Atlanta, who summarized his
views in a news story in these words: "God created the world
and ruled over past history. Revolutionary changes have swept
away the world and its God. Christians must accept God's
death and get on with their faith in Christ, expressed in words
and concepts today's world can understand." Why he wants
us to "get on with our faith" in one who, in his view, was apparently deluded, is as confusing to me as the language with
which he proposes be used so the world can understand. I hope
the world understands what Altizer is saying better than I
can. For, I am frank to confess I just don't know what he
means. But if we are to turn from a dead God to a living Christ,
then we are asked to put our hope in one who never once
questioned the fact of God's vital aliveness in life and the
world. Yet this theological fad—I refuse to dignify it by calling
it a school of thought—would have us reject the Jesus concept
that God is alive and accept the fact that the God of Jesus is
dead.

As a matter of fact, one cannot understand Jesus and his
teaching without accepting the fact that he based his whole
life—and ours—on the confident hope that God is living and
vital reality. Could Jesus have been talking about a dead God
when he said to his disciples, "For men it is impossible, but
not for God; anything is possible for God"? I think not. The
God of Jesus is not dead.

I share the concern of today's theologians for a fresh rendering of the words of our faith so they will be relevant to modern man. I share their concern for the weak kinds of belief in God which have reduced him in power and vitality until there is no strength in him. God has ceased to exist as a vital force in the lives of these who hold such watered-down beliefs. I am certain that the fact that God is alive or dead would make little conscious difference to many Americans. They live as if God didn't exist. The announcement of his funeral would come with little surprise element.

But, I choose to accept what Jesus declared about God, rather than what a few men of admitted intellectual competence in other areas would tell me about my need to be a "Christian atheist." I call your attention to three things that clearly are a part of Jesus' thought about God. He was certain of God's existence. He was aware of the nature of God. He was faithful in doing God's will.

Jesus Was Certain of God's Existence

You scan the scriptures in vain to find one word attributed to Jesus in which he seeks to prove the existence of God. He assumed the existence of God and went on from there. He assumed it for himself and for others who were attracted by his teachings. He said to his disciples, "You believe in God, believe also in me."

Now, admittedly, such faith and confidence may not be enough for today's intellectual who seeks proof of God's existence in order fully to affirm God in his life. And, man across the centuries has sought to find and proclaim this kind of proof. In the field of science there have always been those who have linked up their findings with the Ultimate Reality of the universe. They may have used some other term than "God" but the reference was precisely the same.

Take the astronomer, F. R. Moulton. Years ago he wrote, "To an astronomer the most remarkable thing about the stellar universe is not its vast extent in space, nor the long periods of astronomical time, nor the violence of the forces that operate within the stars. The thing that strikes the astronomer with awe is the perfect orderliness of celestial phenomena. From the tiny satellites of the solar system to the vast galaxy of our stars and the other immense galaxies beyond, there is no sign of chaos. There is nothing haphazard, nothing capricious. *The orderliness of the universe is the supreme discovery of science.*" Begin there in your search for the certainty of a divine creative power which has produced a world of law and order and beauty.

A tourist was once crossing the desert with his Arab guide. He marveled at the old man's faith, for the Arab daily took time out to pray several times along the journey. "Why do you pray to someone whom you cannot see?" asked the tourist. "How can you be sure there really is a God?"

The old man did not answer immediately, but the next day as they traveled along, he answered with another question: "Last night as we were in our tents, we heard a noise. How do you know that camels passed by?" The man replied, "Because this morning I saw the footprints of the camels." The wise old Arab smiled knowingly, and said,

"Likewise do I know there is a God. When I see the beauty of the fiery sky, when I drink from the cooling waters of the green oasis, when I behold the stars in the heavens above, I know that these were created by a Master Craftsman. I know there is a God because I see his footprints everywhere."

And that expression is echoed by many a modern scientists. An article in the *Pulpit Digest* related that a minister asked the Harvard scientist Kirtley Mather if he still would make the statement he made many years ago, "We live in a universe, not of chance or caprice, but of law and order." His reply was, "I *not* only will not repudiate it, but I would underscore it as even truer than it was when first I wrote it."

Dr. Albert Einstein was speaking in the same vein, shortly before his death, when he said, "Certain it is that a conviction, akin to religious feeling, of the rationality or intelligibility of the world lies behind all scientific work of a higher order."

Jesus and the biblical writers would hold that one does not need this kind of proof of design, purpose, and orderliness in the universe in order to accept the fact of a divine author and creator. William Barclay comments that they would have said that a man no more needs to prove that God exists than he needs to prove that his wife exists. He meets his wife every day and he meets God every day. As one professor commented about the announcement of the so-called "death of God," "It cannot be, for I know he is *not* dead. I just spoke to him this morning."

But if we were to try to prove that God exists, using our own minds to do so, how would we proceed? We could begin from the world where we now live. A man named Paley once advanced an argument which is still timely in this regard. Suppose a man walking along a road strikes his foot against a watch lying in the dust. He never has before, in his life, seen a watch. He has no idea what it is. He picks it up. He sees that it consists of a metal case, and inside he finds a complicated arrangement of wheels, levers, springs, and jewels. He finds that the whole thing is moving and working in an orderly fashion. He notes further that the hands are moving around the dial in an obviously predetermined routine. What does he then say? Does he conclude, "All these metals and jewels came together from the ends of the earth by chance, by chance made themselves into this mechanism, by chance wound themselves up and set themselves going, by chance acquired their obvious orderly working? "No, indeed. He says, 'I have found a watch; somewhere there must be a watchmaker.' " Similarly, we look at the world and we are bound to declare, "Somewhere there must be a worldmaker."

Read what Charles A. Lindbergh wrote during his historic flight across the Atlantic more than forty years ago, "It's hard to be an agnostic up here in the Spirit of St. Louis, aware of the frailty of man's devices, a part of the universe between its earth and stars. If one dies, all this goes on existing in a plan so perfectly balanced, so wonderfully simple, so incredibly complex that it's far beyond our comprehension—worlds and moons revolving; planets orbiting on suns; suns flung with apparent recklessness through space. There's the infinite magnitude of the universe; there's the infinite detail of its matter

—the outer star, the inner atom. And man conscious of it all —a worldly audience to what if not to God?"

And we in our present age, when man has conquered space, put men on the moon and opened a whole new vista of vision for every man, have heard similar testimony from astronauts, both during and after their long journeys.

Jesus was not only certain of God's existence, but he acknowledged many times the fact that he could not get along without a conscious awareness of God. Jesus constantly was referring to his need for God. There are some who will accept the existence of God as an impersonal being of power, but they assume they have no need for God in their conscious lives. Tracey Jones tells of a London minister who called on a family in an apartment house. The daughter in the family opened the door and when she saw the visitor's clerical collar said flatly, "We don't need God. We have everything we need." She then shut the door in the parson's face.

Yet, Jesus' conscious need of God is a common need among men. One finds validation for this conclusion among psychiatrists, for example. Here is Dr. Viktor Frankl of Vienna who said, "To deny the spiritual side of one's nature does it great violence . . . Men and women are driven not only by sex and ambition, but also by an overriding need for God. They must overcome the modern-day notion that religion and God are not real needs."

You may claim that God is dead. You may deny the existence of God. But you cannot use Jesus as an authority for such denial. Jesus was certain of God's existence. In fact, he said, "Anything is possible for God."

39

Jesus Learned the Nature of God

Part of our problem in understanding God and gaining certainty as to his existence is the limitation of our human minds. The human mind can never fully know what God is like. We have to gain our centainty within the human limitations. St. Augustine was one of the early church fathers. One day he was walking along the seashore in meditation. He was thinking about the doctrine of the Trinity and asking the questions we often ask: How could God be three—and yet be one? His attention was drawn to a little girl playing on the beach. Back and forth she went from sea to shore. With each returning trip she carried a shovel full of water from the ocean to a little hole she had dug. In response to his inquiry as to what she was trying to do, she replied with childlike confidence, "Oh, I am going to empty the sea into this little hole I've dug."

Augustine reported that he resumed his walk and his thought. Then he said to himself, "I am trying to do exactly what that little girl is doing—trying to crowd the infinite God into this finite mind of mine." No, we must accept the limitations of our humanity in trying to understand the nature of God.

There is also the danger that we will end up with a lopsided view of God. You'll remember the fable of the blind men and the elephant. None had ever seen one, and each concluded that the elephant resembled the particular part of the animal which he happened to touch. One thought an elephant looked like a wall because he touched his huge side. Another touched a leg and concluded he was like a tree. Another grasped the tail and announced an elephant is like a rope. Each was partially correct, but each was substantially wrong.

In seeking to know the nature of God, we may find ourselves emphasizing one aspect or another of his nature to the exclusion of others. Here is the person who insists that God is "wholly Other"—he is transcendant, outside our realm of understanding, experience, and observation. Someone else insists that God is not "out there" but is within. He is all "nearness" for this person. Someone will see God only as a stern Judge whose justice is administered without thought to mercy and he will bow before this Judge in abject fear. Another will remove the firing pin of judgment and reduce God only to flabby, grandfatherly benevolence. Such blind men insist that they have the full story on the appearance of this divine elephant. Actually, they are partially correct, but in their lopsided views they are substantially incorrect.

This is why it is important for us to listen to Jesus when he talks about his understanding of the nature of God. He had a balanced picture of God.

Jesus thought of God as a *Merciful Judge.* He left little question but that God does indeed judge us according to our sins, but he understood that judgment to be tempered with mercy and the spirit of forgiveness.

Jesus thought of God as *Creative Power,* the author of the universe, but the creator of the dynamic quality of the spiritual life of man as well.

Jesus thought of God as *Eternal Goodness.* Whatever explanation one might have for the dark side of the world, for the evil in men's hearts and in the world around us—for Jesus, God is to be identified with ultimate goodness. He wills only the good for his children. He seeks only their fulfillment of a purpose which is basically goodness in nature.

Fully to understand what Jesus believed to be the nature of God, one must see that Jesus regarded God as *Heavenly Father*. He constantly spoke of God as Father and he regularly spoke to God as Father. If you can take all the good concepts that cluster around the idea of a loving earthly father and attach them to your idea of God, you will approximate something of what Jesus apparently had in mind when he said of God, "Our Father who art in heaven." It is in and through Jesus that we can come to know about the nature of God. We know he is good, he is loving, he is redeeming, because this is what Jesus believed God to be. Jesus taught us that we can safely assume that the heart of the world is a heart of fatherly love.

It doesn't take theological sophistication to know this. Recall that scene in Marjorie Kinnan Rawlings' novel, *The Yearling*. Here is the story of primitive and backwoods people in a remote section of Florida. A pitiful figure in the story is a crippled, half-witted boy named Fodder-Wing. In spite of his mental and physical handicaps, he had a way with animals. The wild creatures in the forests of the Everglades became his friends. He enjoyed their company and seemed through them to find a fulfillment in life which was denied him because of his twisted mind and body. One day Fodder-Wing died. His body lay in the rough, handmade burying box and the family and friends gathered for the funeral. There was no preacher among them. But, everyone thought something religious should be said and they called on Penny, a strong and purposeful man to say the words, "Penny, you've had a Christian raising. We'd be proud did you say somethin'."

Standing at the open grave, with his face lifted to the sun, Penny prayed:

"O Lord, Almighty God. Hit ain't for us ignorant mortals to say what's right and what's wrong. Was ary one of us to be a'doin' of it, we'd not of brung this pore boy into the world a cripple, and his mind teched. We'd of brung him in straight and tall like his brothers, fitten to live and work and do. But in a way of speakin', Lord, you done made it up to him. You give him a way with the wild creeturs. You give him a sort o' wisdom, made him knowin' and gentle. The birds come to him, and the varmints moved free about him, and like as not he could o' takened a she wildcat right in his pore twisted hands.

"Now you've done seed fit to take him where bein' crookedy in mind or limb don't matter. But Lord, it pleasures us to think now you've done straightened out them legs and that pore bent back and them hands. Hit pleasures us to think on him, movin' around as easy as ary one. And Lord, give him a few red-birds and mebbe a squirrel and a 'coon and a 'possum to keep him comp'ny, like he had it here. All of us is somehow lonesome and we know he'll not be lonesome, do he have them leetle wild things around him, if it ain't askin' too much to put a few varmints in Heaven. Thy will be done. Amen." [1]

Jesus said, "For man it is impossible, but not for God; anything is possible for God." Jesus believed that. Penny believed that. Do you believe that?

Jesus Told Us What We Can Expect of God

Much of the uncertainty about God which plagues people today is based on his apparent failure to fulfill expectations. We will speak more of this when we talk about prayer. But in this context we need to suggest that we may not be looking for the right things when we draw up our list of expectations.

People have a way of anticipating that someone can do more for them than he himself knows he can. Gwyn Thomas, the Welsh novelist, has recently written an autobiography in which he recounts his varied experiences and wanderings, and the disillusionments that led him to return to his native Rhondda Valley in Wales. He had been a misfit student of medieval Spanish literature, first at Oxford and then in Republican Madrid. He was a social worker, a teacher, and a writer of novels, plays, and essays that have won him a growing band of enthusiastic followers. For a Welshman, he achieved what one critic called "the ultimate popular canonization as an intellectual" when he became a member of the august Brains Trust of the British Broadcasting Company. This exposed him to a wide audience as a pundit, a pontificater on a wide range of unlike subjects. But it had its price. For the "voters" back home credited him with a kind of divine omniscience and they showered him with requests for information. "They would demand from me the winner of the Derby or the whereabouts of a pigeon or a wife that had failed to return to the loft. I would tell them." Because he was knowledgeable in so many areas, people crowned him with a kind of superhuman ability to provide information which no man could provide.

How many would-be Christians have been disillusioned at this point. They expect things from God which Jesus never expected. They assume a kind of pipeline from heaven which will flow regularly with the answers to whatever needs they may imagine God should satisfy.

What then can we expect of God? What hopes can we sustain in this regard? The best summary answer I have found was given by Ernest Fremont Tittle in the volume that became his valedictory. He was completing the final editing in 1949 when he died at his desk. It is a commentary on the Gospel of Luke. In it he has this to say:

What may we reasonably expect of God—the God of the Christian faith? We may expect God to maintain an order of nature that is all-essential for our existence and our welfare; we may not expect him to violate natural law in order to save us from bodily harm or death. We may expect God to maintain the moral order of the world; we may not expect him to intervene between our sins and their natural consequences. We may expect God to maintain among men the power of choice, which is a necessary condition of personal life; we may not expect him to save us from total war by coercing us into doing "the things that make for peace." We may expect God to maintain the interrelatedness of men and of nations, since this means the opportunity for love and fellowship, and the possibility of advance in knowledge, in civilization, and in the arts and sciences and religion; we may not expect him to intervene for the protection of the innocent when men and nations run amuck. Life shared with others inevitably involves that the suffering entailed by sin and folly will not be confined to the guilty. We may expect God to seek at all times our greatest good; but this does not necessarily mean that we shall be spared loss and pain. He who "did not spare his own Son but gave him up for us all" (Rom. 8:32) may call upon his trusted servants to do things necessary for the world's redemption that involve no little risk and cost.[2]

Such expectations of God can bring greater certainty into our faith.

Jesus Was Faithful in Doing God's Will

If we are to trust the New Testament report of the beliefs and actions of Jesus, then we are not long in learning that Jesus believed one should always do the will of God. How often he emphasized that "My will is to do the will of the Father who sent me." When one asks what God is like, the best answer the Christian can give is, "Look at Jesus and you will see what God is like." Bishop McConnell popularized for us the phrase "the Christlike God," as a means of pointing up this answer. All that is Christ-like is God-like. All that one finds in Jesus' life and thought is what God wills to be found in every life and thought.

Much of Jesus' life was spent in the prayerful search for understanding what God's will for his life really was. I stood

[2] Ernest F. Tittle, *The Gospel According to Luke* (New York: Harper, 1951), pp. 165-66.

46

one day at the place in the Jordan River which is traditionally held to be the site of Jesus' baptism. Yonder I could see beyond the river the desert into which Jesus went immediately thereafter to experience what we know as his desert temptations. My guide pointed off in the distance toward Jericho and beyond to the Mount of the Temptations. And in that original setting, it was not difficult to picture Jesus, face to face with the challenge of his call of God, leaving the crowds and going alone to meditate on this divine summons. What did it mean to be the Messiah? How could he best fulfill God's call on his life? What was God's will for him in terms of the methods and means for bringing his message to men? There in that desert he charted the course for his ministry. And the compass was then and always would be "the will of my Heavenly Father." That Jesus' determination of this course needed shoring up is clearly seen in his frequent returns to the lonely place of prayer. It was this mountaintop, that garden, this corner of the temple—any spot where he could in quietness and confidence turn to God in prayer. He found through this experience of communion with the Father, just what was the will of God for his life for that moment. And then, in the moments of prayer, Jesus would linger long enough to gain the divine strength to go forth and do that will.

We too can know God's will. We have the example of Jesus. We have the assurance from him that what he learned, we can learn. As he lived in fellowship with the Father, we too could live in fellowship with God. We explain away our failures by the fact that we cannot know what God's will is for us. Yet, is that really the cause of our failure? Is it not true

47

that many times we do indeed know God's will for us, but our failure is in not doing that will? Leslie Weatherhead pointed this up when he said, "Usually what one needs is not discernment but grit. For myself, more than I need discernment, I need fortitude, courage, faith, determination and perseverance. Not to see, merely to do." And Dan Walker, commenting on this, pointed out that Jesus did *not* say, "not my will but thine be *known*," but rather he did say, "not my will but thine be *done*."

How much easier it is to fail to seek God's will. We feel less guilty when we haven't tried to learn God's will, for we remember the last time when clearly we knew what God wanted but we didn't do it and we felt so guilt-ridden about it. Hans Denk has given it worthy expression in these words, "O my God, how does it happen in this poor old world that Thou art so great and yet nobody finds Thee, that Thou callest so loudly and nobody hears Thee, that Thou art so near and nobody feels Thee, that Thou givest Thyself to everybody and nobody knows Thy name. Men flee from Thee and say they cannot find Thee; they turn their backs and say they cannot see Thee; they stop their ears and say they cannot hear Thee."

Our Christian faith tells us that to know Jesus Christ is to know God and that his will in life is not an imponderable or an unknown. It is discernible for every man. It is knowable by every one of us. We can look to Jesus Christ and find in him and through him the assurance of the existence of God, and an awareness of the nature of God which helps us know what God is like, and we can pattern our lives after the life of Jesus who was faithful in doing the will of God.

Dr. Harold A. Bosley took part in a radio interview in St. Louis in connection with a study conference of the National Council of Churches in 1966. He assumed his questioner would concentrate on the many serious problems of our day to be considered by that conference—Vietnam, Cuba, China. He reports real surprise when the first question concerned "the death of God." His radio host asked Dr. Bosley, "But is God really dead?" The minister reports he was tempted to ask, "What difference would it make to you, personally, this very minute, if I should answer, 'Yes, God is dead, really dead?'" Well we can wonder what difference it would have made in terms of his life and his work, his problems and his dreams, his hopes and his values.

But let's get personal with the question. What difference would it make to you if you believed, really believed, that God is dead?

However, if we are to accept Jesus' word, then we can believe that God is not dead, but very much alive. So, let's ask a similar question, "What difference would it make in your life if you believed, really believed, that God is alive?"

God Cares—Love

What would you say is mankind's most persistent question? What is the question which keeps recurring in every generation? Would you agree it is this simple question: "What is God like?" That question persists because the way one answers that question determines not only the other answers, but also the other questions you ask.

In search of such an answer, where would you go to find it in a single statement? There are many biblical statements which might qualify. It seems to be answered best in the first Letter of John. The author states very simply: "God is love." Richard Niebuhr comments in *Christ and Culture,* "This little classic (I John) has been treasured by Christians for its profound understanding and beautiful statement of the doctrine of love. It achieves the simple summary of Christian theology: 'God is love,' and the equally concise formulation of Christian ethics: 'Love one another.' It presents in their inseparable relation and in fugue-like manner the three themes of love: God's love for man, and man's love for God, and brother's for brother."

I John summarizes the full impact of what "God is love" means in words that tell of the incarnation of that divine love in the person of Jesus. "This is how God showed his love for us: he sent his only Son into the world that we might have life through him." (4:9) God cares for us so much that he has come to us in Christ to meet our needs through this fullest expression of his divine love.

In his novel *The Heart of the Matter,* Graham Greene tells the story of an English chief of police in Africa. He is a frustrated man. He is bitter and involved "in a tangled web of intrigue, adultery and murder." He is driven to despair and thinks about committing suicide. He has abandoned religion, yet "in a gesture of defiance he goes into the church for the last time, more to damn God than to pray." But the spirit of God envelops him, and he cries out, "How desperately God must love me!" Precisely! God is our Father, said Jesus. We are God's children. He loves us in spite of what we may have done with ourselves.

What I hear John saying about this is simply that we cannot really know God until we know him as love and speak of him as love. A recent English writer, D. W. D. Shaw, puts it, "all our data for reality—the story which scripture has to tell, the historical experience of the Church, even our own ex-

51

perience of what is real in our personal life with other persons—impel us to speak of God realistically in terms of love." "God loved the world so much that he gave his only Son, that everyone who has faith in him may not die but have eternal life." (John 3:16 NEB.)

Love in the Human Scene

Some years ago Elton Trueblood received a letter from a former student. He wrote, "I have become a new man in the classless revolution—a loyal believer of Marx-Leninism—I cannot longer address you as a religious brother, but I send you my revolutionary love." It may be difficult for us to equate love with the Communist revolution. But it certainly is clear that God's love makes some very revolutionary changes in the human scene when we strive to make it alive in human relationships.

To be sure, it is no easy task to talk about love, particularly the love of God. The word love has come to have so many different connotations in our time. It is used to speak of that emotion which is sheer sentimentality. We speak of a love story in a novel or on the screen—a love epic, we say. Yet, we mean sentimental, romantic love, most of the time. We don't know what other word to use. Like the sailor who sent a telegram to his girl friend from his port of embarkation. He simply scribbled "I love you, I love you, I love you" on the telegram blank. The clerk read it and told him he could send one more word at no additional cost. So he added the word "love."

Or we limit our use of the word to our emotional feelings in the area of sex. Sexual love is not only a natural kind of experience, it is basically an honorable one. Yet, there is more to love—even between a husband and wife—than the sex act.

There is the love which we share with members of our family, with close friends. But haven't you found that this is often a kind of "you scratch my back and I'll scratch yours" affair? Not always consciously, perhaps. But it is love profered with the assumption that it will be returned. It is an investment made with anticipation that there will be dividends.

Eric Fromm has helped us see the differences between mature and immature forms of love as human relationship. He writes in *The Art of Loving,* "Love is not primarily a relationship to a specific person; it is an attitude, an orientation of character which determines the relatedness of a person to the world as a whole, not toward one 'object' of love." He goes on to say, "Infantile love follows the principle 'I love because I am loved.' Mature love follows the principle 'I am loved because I love.' Immature love says: 'I love you because I need you.' Mature love says: 'I need you because I love you.'"

The Greeks had more than a word for love. They had four words, as a matter of fact. Each of them offers a facet of what the world calls love. *Eros* is the love of a man for a woman. It implies passion. Incidentally, it does not appear in the New Testament. *Philia* is the word for brotherly love. It expresses our love for those who are nearest and dearest to us. *Storge* means affection. It has reference particularly to parental love and the love of a child for his parents. *Agape* is the love of God incarnate in Christ. It is an unconditional love, an unconquerable benevolence. Barclay, in *The Letters to Galatians and Ephesians,* makes this comment about *agape:* "It means that no matter what a man may do to us by way of insult or injury or humiliation, we will never seek anything else but his highest good. It is therefore a feeling of the mind as much as it is of the heart; it concerns the will just as much as it does the emotions. It describes the deliberate effort—which we can only make with the help of God—never to seek anything but the best even for those who seek the worst for us."

Primarily sentimental, yet pointing to this giving quality are the words from Rodgers and Hammerstein's *Sound of Music.*

> A bell is no bell 'til you ring it,
> A song is no song 'til you sing it,
> And love in your heart, wasn't put there to stay . . .
> Love isn't love 'til you give it away." [1]

Love in Divine Dimension

We cannot know nor experience what love really means in length and breadth and depth and height short of a knowledge of the divine dimension of love which came to us from God in Jesus. Take the "Flower Power" movement among the so-called hippies. They dedicated themselves to love as the ultimate reality, and this became a God-substitute for them. As Shaw states, "Their ultimate reality proved to be an illusion. Their God was their own idea of love, not the God who is love, of the Christian gospel."

[1] Copyright © 1959 by Richard Rodgers and Oscar Hammerstein, II. Used by permission of Williamson Music, Inc.

The Christian gospel teaches that Jesus put content into what is meant by love when we say "God is love." We see the nature of God and his love through that love which God has showed for us in sending his only Son into the world that we might discover what real life-in-love is through him. We can see facets of this diamond of divine love in expressions of three writers.

Theologian Daniel D. Williams commenting on the word *agape* in *God's Grace and Man's Hope* says, "Love is the content of the Kingdom, and it is the power of God's love which brings the world into the Kingdom. Eternal life means life in the eternal love of God. . . . Christ is the restoration of the true image of man, because he is the incarnation of the love which is the meaning of our existence."

Swiss physician, Paul Tournier, has helped us a great deal in understanding the relationship of our Christian faith in developing and maintaining a high level of emotional and mental health. *In Guilt and Grace* he states, "The proclamation of Jesus Christ is about the love of God, a love which is all-inclusive and unconditional."

Ecumenical leader, Albert C. Outler, adds another insight in *Who Trusts in God:* "The world is perishing for lack of the sort of environing love that *is* disinterested, that does not 'intervene' or dominate, that turns men's hearts outward toward the neighbor, that suffers and struggles against man's inhumanity to man. But this is another way of pointing to the very nerve of the Christian tradition: God's *agape,* his love of creation and humanity. All the other modes of God's presence in the world are summed up in this: this *is* what he is!

His *agape* is his motive for providing a world to begin with; his love for the world so provided is what prompted the Incarnation of his love in Jesus Christ."

We must also realize our own human limitations in trying to understand how God is eternal and how his love is something that transcends anything we may have known outside that love. To be sure, we are never "outside God's love" except as we live as if neither God nor his love exists. As James Wallace Hamilton phrased it, "How can we, born yesterday, dying tomorrow with minds that cannot see a day ahead, measure the movements or meaning of a mind that is eternal?" True! Yet, we can gain some insight into the dimensions of this divine love because God has revealed that love to us in Christ. The life we "might have through him" is a life which is grounded in this kind of *agape* love. We must see that God is love, not love is God, else we commit the hippie fallacy of anchoring our love in our personal preference rather than rooting it in the Christian gospel of love.

The dimension of God's love which we call eternal is hard for us to grasp even when we see it revealed in the human scene through Jesus. Our real question is how we can move up from the confines of human finitude in our concept of love only as we grasp the real miracle of love: that God has linked the eternal and the divine with the limited and the human in his revelation of the Divine Nature as basically that of love.

How does this happen? We may find help in the experience of a Cambridge University student whose story was in *The Christian Century*. The magazine writer asked the young man, in a discussion, if he would call himself a Christian. He replied that now he felt he might do so, but added that he would not have done so when he first came to the university. "Why not," he was asked. "My damned school chapel," was his answer. Then he recounted how all he had ever heard in chapel at school was sermonizing of a theological sort, which he couldn't understand, or preaching of a hearty sort about Christ in the Rugby match, which nauseated him, or warning about the perils of masturbation and homosexuality, which infuriated him. "Religious instruction was dates and facts with an occasional bit of rhetoric about how it was Christian faith that had made Britain great."

He reported that what had converted him at Cambridge was Harry Williams probing to the depths of his soul in a sermon he happened to hear. It was Hugh Montefiore's impressing him with his sheer intellectual integrity at the university church on one or two Sunday evenings, his learning that a distinguished scholar who commands international respect was a Christian believer. All that, plus his happening to have a supervisor who helped him find himself academically and personally.

Then his questioner asked, "What do you think Christianity is?" And he answered, "Being willing to risk your life on the belief that it's love that makes the world run." And then the second question, "But however can you believe that?" His reply: "Because Jesus lived it out as love, and I don't believe *he* was wrong."

Isn't that what John was getting at when he wrote, "This

is how God showed his love for us: he sent his only Son into the world that we might have life through him."

God's love is not only eternal, it is universal. Many problems that arise in the human society come because we assume that God's love, and thus his favor is to be confined to the chosen few. Racism rears its ugly head because one race gets the idea that God's love is for it alone. Nationalism becomes a problem between nations when one nation assumes a kind of divine all-knowing attitude which looks down its nose at other nations not so fortunate as to be the recipients of God's love.

The Christian gospel holds that the love of God pervades all the world and is poured out on every person. But it is not so easy to believe in this when you are among the "have nots." Men may be interested in life's meaning, but not at the moment they are struggling simply to survive in a nation or culture where starvation stalks every street and misery makes company of all citizens. As Shaw observes, "proclaiming a message of love in circumstances which speak more eloquently of misery, deprivation, neglect and indifference, with death as a possible escape from meaninglessness—that is a dangerous enterprise."

One of the main answers to this contrast between the world in which the poverty-pocket people exist and the world which should attend persons who are the recipients of God's love is to be found in the fact that men are often the agents through which God's love gets through to needy men. So often, history tells us, human needs have been met by love through human beings who have been transformed by God's love as revealed in Jesus Christ.

58

One can see this simply illustrated in the love of a young man for a young woman. His whole life is transformed when he "falls into love" with her. He wants to do anything that will contribute to her happiness, her welfare, her well-being. No task is too great. No price is too high for him to pay in seeking her good. Anyone who has been in love knows what I'm saying here. Our problem is that we fail to realize fully what it means to be transformed by God's love. To fall into love with God is to seek his will, to do his bidding, to be an agent for extending his *agape* to all those he loves.

The cross tells us there is no limit to God's love for us. We cannot fully experience that love if we fail to seek to knock down the fences around our love. When we do this, then we are ready to be agents for the expression of divine love in the human scene. We may be the person who helps someone else know that God loves him. Thus, we become instruments for the transformation of a life through love. Harriet Beecher Stowe once wrote, "And my theology is, once penetrate any human soul with the full belief that God loves him, and you save him." Through this saving love, a person is introduced to the life which God sent his Son into the world that we might have.

God's love is eternal. It is universal. And, it is moral. Jesus revealed a Heavenly Father who is our God. But Jesus did not even imply, let alone suggest, that God is an easygoing, good-natured grandfather who tolerantly and lovingly smiles at our sins with kindly benevolence as if to say, "Kids will be kids." God's love is merciful and kind, benevolent and understanding of human weakness. But we do injustice to what

Jesus taught us about God's love if we try to remove from it any element of judgment. God's love judges us, as any honest person can testify from his own experience. It judges us and finds us wanting. But, Jesus assured us that this divine love never deserts us because God the Judge is alike God the Loving Father. In tender mercy and forgiving love, he redeems his children who turn to him in penitence and love. "God was in Christ reconciling the world to himself, no longer holding men's misdeeds against them, and (that) he has entrusted us with the message of reconciliation." (II Cor. 5:19 NEB.) And that message is love.

How God Expresses His Love

We can never fully grasp the magnitude nor the depth of God's love brought to us in Jesus. Frederick W. Faber's hymn expresses it well:

> There's a wideness in God's mercy,
> Like the wideness of the sea; . . .
> For the love of God is broader
> Than the measure of man's mind.

The words of John also point out that Jesus can help us see and understand how God's love is expressed. The Christian gospel teaches that Jesus himself is the finest and fullest expression of divine love. How does God express this love in ways that are identifiable to us through Christ?

For one thing, we find it expressed in a *sensitive concern* and a *Father's care.* To be concerned is to seek the welfare of another. To seek such a welfare is to care enough for that person that we are willing to go to any lengths to bring him into the kind of life God has intended him to have in terms of the Christian life. We can know that God is concerned about us, that he seeks our welfare, that he is concerned with our lives. The Psalmist knew this and said so.

> "For he knows our frame;
>   he remembers that we are dust. . . .
>
> "O Lord, thou hast searched me and known me!
> Thou knowest when I sit down and when I rise up;
>   Thou discernest my thoughts from afar.
> Thou searchest out my path and my lying down,
>   and art acquainted with all my ways."
>   Psalms 103:14; 139:1-3

Moreover, Jesus commented on God's care of us as his children. In the Sermon on the Mount he said, "How little faith you have! No, do not ask anxiously 'What are we to eat? What are we to drink? What shall we wear?' All these are things for the heathen to run after, not for you, because your heavenly Father knows that you need them all" (Matt. 6:31-32 NEB).

God's love is expressed in his *identifying compassion.* One can express concern without getting deeply involved with the object of that concern. We can send a Care package, drop a dollar on the offering plate, or authorize a payroll deduction for contribution to the United Fund. Our concern and our money which expresses it will buy just as many dollars worth of care as the next person's. But for concern to move into real compassion involves the kind of giving love which identifies with the recipient of that love.

It is the kind of compassion that prompted St. Francis of Assisi to embrace the leperous beggar who became for him a symbol of all the suffering and poverty-stricken people of the world. He then gave his life in the effort to identify with these brothers and sisters. It is this kind of compassion and divine love which prompted Jesus to look down from the cross and love his enemies, who had put him there, so much that he could intercede for their forgiveness. It was this compassion that through his years of ministry had caused him to identify with all forms of suffering humanity. And, if we believe that God came to us in Christ to reveal his nature as love, then in the compassion of Christ we can see the compassion of a loving Father who is seeking in this fashion to identify himself with humanity.

The cross reveals how completely God is willing to identify with his children. Sacrificial love that suffers is an expression of compassionate concern that identifies with the beloved. And in Christ we have the pattern for our lives.

There is a tender story of a father's love. It took place at the three hundredth anniversary of the University of Dublin. Dr. James Martineau was being honored by the school where he had taught some sixty years before. He was one of England's great religious thinkers, known by many for the beauty of his written prayers. During the days he had lived in Dublin, he and his wife lost a small daughter in death, and she had been buried here. In later years his wife also died. Now at eighty-seven, the lonely old man left the busy scene attending the academic honor and anniversary celebration and went to stand once more in the churchyard beside the grave of his daughter, now sixty years in the Father's house. It is most interesting to note that Dr. Martineau had outlived his peers; and no other living soul recalled that little face. But the father did not forget. Now if that is what a human father is like in his love, then how much more can we expect from the heart of God, the Father of us all? He loves us. He cares for us. He gives us life and sustains that life through his love revealed in Christ. He identifies with us as persons and we know his love in this fashion.

Finally, of course, we find the love of God expressed in his *redeeming covenant.* The Old Testament is the record of a covenant people. They had accepted God as their God under the leadership of Moses during the wilderness wanderings. At their highest and best moments, the people of Israel were in fact God's people. Though they wandered away, God proved faithful and ready to receive them back to himself and to restore them—as individuals or as a nation—to his fellowship. Out of the Old Testament covenant we have the assurance of the faithfulness of God.

Out of the New Testament Covenant we receive assurance of the love of God. Here is a covenant of love which binds the children of earth to the Heavenly Father who is incarnate love and who expressed that love through Christ. Here is redeeming love which gives life in God to all who know him in Christ.

63

Perhaps no book in recent years has recorded the power of this kind of redeeming love when it is accepted and lived in human society as did Ernest Gordon's *Through the Valley of the Kwai,* an account of his experiences in the World War II prisoner-of-war camp on the River Kwai. Here is an account of misery and suffering, torture and horror, starvation and forced labor. Men lived by the law of the jungle—do anything you have to and can do to survive. Here was literal hell on earth until one day a man did an act of unselfishness that denied this law of the jungle. A fellow Scotsman came to Gordon, who had been left by the camp authorities to die. He began to care for him, to bathe the ulcers on his legs, to bring him some of his own food. When asked why he was doing it, Dusty Miller explained that somewhere in the Bible it says this is what one is supposed to do. Word got around the camp about this action.

Then one day a guard was counting the shovels of a detachment of prisoners who had returned from work detail. He announced it was one short. He demanded to know who had hidden it. Finally in frustration, when no one would admit taking it, the guard drew his gun and threatened to shoot them all if the guilty man did not confess. Thereupon, one of the prisoners stepped forward and said he had taken the shovel. Enraged, the guard struck him with his gun and literally beat and kicked him to death. When they returned to the camp the shovels were counted again. None was missing. The death of this man was a transforming influence in Chungkai. Men began to recognize that there was more there than hatred and death, there was love and life. Ernest Gordon wrote, "True there was hatred, but there was also love. There was death, but there was also life. God had not left us. He was with us, calling us to live the divine life in fellowship. I was beginning to feel the miracle that God was working in the Death Camp by the River Kwai."

And this was but the reenactment in the human scene of the miracle of love which came into the world when God was in Christ. "This is how God showed his love for us: he sent his only Son into the world that we might have life through him."

God Gives—Grace

Everything you have in your life was given you by God. Did you create the life-giving air you breathe, or the refreshing water you drink, or any of the food which nourishes your body? All our life is dependent upon God, and all our hope is ultimately founded upon his divine purpose for us which he has revealed to us in Jesus Christ. This basically is our doctrine of God and how he meets our needs. But to see it more clearly, note two vignettes which highlight the fact of God's existence, his grace, and his coming in Christ.

A story is told of a rabbi in a European village, who one day summoned the townspeople to the village square. He said he had an important announcement. The people gathered, but not without much grumbling at the inconvenience. The merchant resented having to leave his business. The housewife complained because she had so many home chores to do. But, in obedience to their rabbi, they went unwillingly to the town square. When all were present, the rabbi said, "I wish to announce there is a God in the world." That was all he said, but his people understood. They knew they had been acting as if God did not actually exist. And the rabbi wanted them to realize that God does exist.

The next vignette is the story, in Gerald Kennedy's *Go Inquire of the Lord,* of a boy who stood looking at the greenhouse in the royal gardens in Sweden. His mother was ill and he wanted so desperately to take her some of the lovely grapes he saw hanging on the vines. At last he mustered up enough courage to ask the gardener if he could buy just one bunch, but he was sternly refused. A young man standing nearby heard the request. He came over, cut off two fine bunches of grapes, and put them in the boy's hand. The boy offered money to pay for them. But, the young man, who was the prince, refused the payment. He said, "My father is not a merchant who sells; he is a king who gives."

When you wade through all the theology which seeks to interpret our Christian faith in God, you come out in about the same place as you do with these two instances. They tell us that God is, that his grace meets our needs because he is a king who loves and gives, whether or not we deserve his gifts.

The Apostle Paul had much to say about the grace of God. He, himself, had experienced so much of God's loving goodness and generous love. He reminded the Christians in

Ephesus that they had not earned their relationship with God. It was his gift to them. "For it is by his grace you are saved, through trusting him; it is not your own doing. It is God's gift, not a reward for work done" (Eph. 2:8 NEB). And so we sing about it in the old Methodist camp-meeting hymn:

> Amazing grace! how sweet the sound
> That saved a wretch like me!
>
> The Lord has promised good to me,
> His word my hope secures;
> He will my shield and portion be
> As long as life endures.

Grace—God's Gift

The biblical usage of the word "grace" has reference to God's disposition to show favor to sinful man. The *Encyclopedia of Religion* states: "For the Christian believes with the apostle Paul that when men were without strength or even the will to save themselves, God's unrestrained kindness interposed and salvation is now freely offered them through the crucified and risen Christ." As Paul wrote to the Roman Christians, "Therefore, now that we have been justified through faith, let us continue at peace with God through our Lord Jesus Christ, through whom we have been allowed to enter the sphere of God's grace, where we now stand. Let us exult in the hope of the divine splendor that is to be ours." (Rom. 5:1-2 NEB.)

In Charles Duthie's words, "At the center of our faith is

the conviction that God is entirely loving, holy and good." The grace of a God who is not loving, who is not always holy, who is morally capricious and ethically undependable would be of little consequence to us. But when we accept the fact that the God who has "promised good to me" is himself a God of goodness; when the God who calls men to holiness and Christian perfection, is himself a God of holiness and perfection; when the God who calls us to put love first in our hearts and the active love of the Christian first in our practice is himself a God whose property is always to have mercy because he, himself, is the God of love—then the grace of God has real impact on our minds and widespread acceptance in our human experience.

Various theologians have given us definitions of the grace of God. Some of them are involved and obtuse. The clearest and most simply stated definition I have found is in an adult study book by John B. Magee. "Grace means that God has accepted us in spite of our sins and failures and secured for us a loving relationship to him. He came to us in Jesus Christ to let us know that our relationship to him is not based upon some merit system, but upon his unlimited love. This is the meaning of Paul's remark that this has happened 'while we were yet sinners.'"

It is not always easy for me to understand what Paul Tillich has written. Yet, in the area of thought about God's grace, he has been most helpful with his concept of acceptance. Speaking of when and how grace comes into man's experience, Tillich wrote in *The Shaking of the Foundations,* "Grace strikes us when we are in great pain and restlessness. It strikes us when we walk through the dark valley of a meaningless and empty life. It strikes us when we feel that our separation is deeper than usual because we have violated another life, a life which we loved, or from which we were estranged. It strikes us when our disgust for our own being, our indifference, our weakness, our hostility, and our lack of direction and composure have become intolerable to us. It strikes us when, year after year, the longed-for perfection of life does not appear, when the old compulsions reign within us as they have for decades, when despair destroys all joy and courage. Sometimes at that moment a wave of light breaks into our darkness, and it is as though a voice were saying: "You are accepted. You are accepted, accepted by that which is greater than you and the name of which you do not know. Do not ask for the name now; perhaps you will find it later. Do not try to do anything now; perhaps later you will do much. Do not seek for anything; do not perform anything; do not intend anything. Simply accept the fact that you are accepted. If that happens to us, we experience grace."

Grace, which is God's gift to us, is given its fullest and finest expression in Jesus Christ. Paul's main thrust in his theological preaching was the fact that Jesus became the instrument whereby God's love and grace were made known to man. Paul said, "For all alike have sinned, and are deprived of the divine splendour, and all are justified by God's free grace alone, through his act of liberation in the person of Christ Jesus." (Rom. 3:23-24 NEB). For the Christian then, grace is a synonym for God's love. A. T. Mollegen states in the *Handbook of Christian Theology*, "The attitude of spontaneous, uncaused favor with which God regards man, expresses itself fully in the life, words, deeds, death and resurrection of Jesus of Nazareth."

Faith—Man's Acceptance

Faith is man's response to God's gift of life and love in Christ. If grace is to be fully received, it must find ready and full acceptance by man. Life becomes a constant affirmation of God's goodness and a perpetual voicing of our gratitude for God's love. A friend and university professor of economics, Dr. Kenneth Boulding, has written some helpful lines:

> My Lord, Thou art in every breath I take,
> And every bite and sup taste firm of Thee.
> With buoyant mercy Thou enfoldest me,
> And holdest up my foot each step I make.
> Thy touch is all around me when I wake,
> Thy sound I hear, and by Thy Light I see
> The world is fresh with Thy Divinity
> And all thy creatures flourish for Thy sake.[1]

Paul Tournier reported in *Guilt and Grace* some conversations he had been having with a Roman Catholic priest, who had been "severely tested by inner conflicts, a restless and tormented man, incredibly clear-sighted about himself and fully conscious of his doubts, rebelliousness and hesitations, and of the profound gloom into which he had been plunged."

---

[1] From *There Is a Spirit, The Nayler Sonnets* (Nyack, N.Y.: Fellowship Publications, 1945), p. 13.

Said the priest, "Yet all of that, nevertheless, in no way shakes my calm certainly of faith and of grace." Then Dr. Tournier goes on to comment in words that might be your testimony as it could be mine, "I feel myself closely akin to that man, in a deep community of spirit. I completely understand him. For though less tried by life, I also for my part am both heavy and light-hearted, sad and joyous, utterly sad and utterly joyous, weak and strong, tormented by guilt for innumerable things and yet confident of the grace of God, not for later on but now in the present." Sounds very much like the Apostle Paul!

Later the Swiss doctor goes on to point out that it is not always easy for us to accept the gift of God's grace. A patient reported to Dr. Tournier her problems at this point, "In the last resort this (God bestowing favors without merit) wounds our self-love, this receiving of what we do not deserve. And this is why we have difficulty in accepting it. We would prefer to have merited it: we contend with God for the merit." What a paradox this presents! We yearn for what God's love and grace alone can provide for us. Yet, we are reluctant to accept it because we have done nothing to merit it.

We need also to see here that while no good works are required in order to receive God's grace, yet the authentic receiver who knows he is accepted of God, will find good works resulting from this acceptance. Paul did not intend that we should assume that the relationship is merely an active one on God's side and a passive reception of God's love on man's side. Theologian Daniel D. Williams expressed it this way: "Grace is not merely the sheer mercy of God descending upon man apart from any moral demand or human effort . . . a doctrine of grace which destroys the freedom and moral responsibility of man is not the grace known in mature Christian experience. The New Testament emphasis is upon grace as forgiveness but never as a substitute for repentance in its ethical dimensions."

William Barclay adds another facet to this fact of faith when he points out that all the good works in the world cannot put us right with God. "But once we have been put right with God there is something radically wrong with the Christianity which does not issue in good works."

A thoroughly delightful little book has been produced by Sister Corita and Joseph Pintauro with the title *To Believe in God*. In simple but moving prose and poetry, with the background of Sister Corita's dramatic art work on each page, the book helps one summarize his belief in God and what it means for human life. In one place the poet writes about a basic meaning of God's grace when he says, "To believe in God is to have somebody who knows you thru and thru and likes you still and all."

But, perhaps you are asking just now, "So much for the theological implications. I want to know just what it is that God's grace and my response in faith does in my life?" Let me put it in several summary sentences.

This all means that our hearts are won by God's love. We are not too far away from the day when you would comment about two persons who were in love and were planning to be married, by saying, "He won her heart with his love." You know precisely what that means, and if you can lift it to the divine dimension you can gain a bit of insight into what Paul was talking about in God's gracious love which is given us as his unconditional gift. But it has meaning for our lives only when we accept that gift and allow our hearts to be won by God's love.

Again, this means that we go through an experience in which our eyes are opened to God by our response of faith. No heart is won without a positive response on the part of its possessor. I inquired one day of a young couple, who were permitting me to share in the planning of their marriage, how they had met. The young man blurted out that they had gone to school together for many years, but they had started dating only after they had graduated from high school. "He didn't even know I existed," she exclaimed. And he replied, "But when I did realize she existed, man alive, it sure changed my life!" And you know what he meant by that! His eyes were opened to beauty, to personality, and to love which he had not before seen—though he had seen her every day at school. God's grace is here and now available for you. You cannot see, let alone accept it, until your eyes are opened by the response of faith.

Moreover, this means for us that our own personal experience will prove the reliability of God's grace. When your heart is won by God's love and your eyes opened by the response of your faith to that love, you will suddenly see your past life in a different perspective. You will note the times when God's grace has carried you without your realizing it, when God's providence has guided your pilgrimage through life even though you were unaware of it. Howard Thurman, in *The*

Growing Edge, tells about the experience of Dr. Richard Cabot of Boston who once gave a lecture on the wisdom of the body which illustrates this point. In a Boston hospital where he was serving, a man died in the outpatient ward following a very bad accident. He was seventy years of age. His wife, grieving over him, said to Dr. Cabot, "Think of it. I have known him since we were little children four or five years old and he has never been sick a day in his life." The doctor explained to the wife that he had never performed an autopsy on a person who had never been sick, would she permit an autopsy. She agreed. The doctor discovered a number of very surprising things. For one thing, he discovered that the man had had tuberculosis for a long time; but nature had so built walls around the tubercle bacilli that they leaked no poison into the bloodstream. The man had been a bartender. He didn't drink; but for forty-five years he had been a "taster" with the result that his liver showed serious affects from alcohol. But he did not know he had that problem. And Dr. Cabot went on to tell of a number of other serious ailments of which the man was unaware because his body had produced in each instance a creative and redemptive element that sealed off these threats to his life and health.

A look at almost any life now in mid-age would find a similar list of discoveries of times and places where God's love and grace worked their silent miracle of healing and sustenance—physically, emotionally, and spiritually.

Finally, grace leads a person through his response of faith into the desire as a Christian to will only the will and purpose of God. Through this combination of grace and faith God's will and purpose becomes our own will and purpose. And in doing God's will we find our peace. At the heart of all of this is the fact that God's love for us is unchanging, it is unconditional, it is poured out on all of us without regard to our merit or our spiritual achievements. And it is always there waiting for our acceptance.

A man in the middle years of life tells of the turning point in his youth. It came at a time when he had been arrested for a serious crime. He had been rebellious of home and parents and now, of society. After he had been booked at the police station his father was called. The father came immediately to the station not knowing any of the facts other than that his son had been arrested on a serious charge. When he arrived, he immediately asked the sergeant if he could speak privately to his son. Permission was granted. In a corner of the court room the father faced the boy who fully expected a dressing down and perhaps would be disowned. However, here's what the grown man recalls his father said: "Son, before I hear any details of why you are here, I want you to know that I love you more than my own life. Nothing you have done will ever change that love I have for you. I don't know what you have done, and I cannot condone it if it is a serious breach of behavior. But I promise you that whatever happens from this night on, I will stand by you all the way."

The man reports that that word from his father marked the turning point in his life. Feeling unworthy of being loved by his father whom he had humiliated with his action, assuming he was to be forever unacceptable in his father's house, he learned the meaning of love and grace.

Is there a better way to describe God's love for us. Are there more adequate words for telling his grace? How better explain God's redeeming forgiveness which accepts us as we are when we respond in faith? God loved the world so much he gave his Son to be our Saviour! "For it is by his grace you are saved, through trusting him; it is not your own doing. It is God's gift, not a reward for work done."

God Saves—Salvation

Every person is haunted by feelings of frustration in his ability to see what is good and his inability to do it, along with his ability to recognize wrong but his inability to refrain from doing it. A man was church-hopping, visiting around trying to find one that suited him, and he happened to come into a church service during the Prayer of Confession. He heard the people saying, "We have done those things we ought not to have done and we have left undone the things we ought to have done." He sat back and relaxed and said to himself: "I have found my church home; here are folks just like myself. These are my kind of people!"

So, all of us are in search of our salvation. We know what we need. But, sometimes we may look in the wrong places for it. We soon learn in life that we cannot save ourselves by our own power. We need someone or something beyond ourselves. The manager of a ten-story office building was informed that an elevator was stalled between the fifth and sixth floors with a man trapped in it. He rushed to the grillwork and called to the passenger, "Keep cool sir, we'll have you out of there in no time. I have phoned for the elevator mechanic." There was a brief pause. Then a tense voice answered from within the elevator, "I am the elevator mechanic." In such a situation he was incapable of saving himself. And so are we in the testing times of life as well as in the times when life flows pretty evenly.

Nor can we trust man alone to save us ultimately. In matters of ultimate reality, man's power is not enough. Recall the story of the Barber's Convention. A public relations agent went down to Chicago's skid row and picked up the sorriest looking specimen of gutter bum. He was taken to the convention hotel. The barber shop gave him the full treatment. The haberdashery outfitted him in the latest clothing. He looked so fine that news photographers, who had been thoughtfully alerted, had a field day with the "before and after" pictures. The hotel manager was so impressed he gave the derelict a job. But the next morning the man didn't show up. They waited a day and then decided to try to locate him. They found him in the same gutter where they had found him before. The hotel man, disillusioned, commented, "The barbers were able to clean him up on the outside, but you can never make anything out of a man until you also change him on the inside." That takes more than human power and ingenuity alone.

To be ultimately saved requires not only the power of God but it takes a positive action on our part as well. Too often we stop too soon. Claudius, the king in Shakespeare's *Hamlet,* faces such reality when he says,

> My fault is past. But, O, what form of prayer
> Can serve my turn? 'Forgive me my foul murder'?
> That cannot be; since I am still possess'd
> Of those effects for which I did the murder,
> My crown, mine own ambition and my queen.
> May one be pardon'd and retain the offence?

Who doubts that the answer to that question must be a re-sounding "No!" One cannot achieve the life he seeks until he is willing to take positive steps to break with the past. We must do all within our power to correct the wrong we have done and change our attitudes and actions toward the right.

This, I maintain, cannot be done without the power of God in our human life. God alone can provide the kind of salvation which saves and redeems us from life that is unhappy, lost, and purposeless.

The Apostle Paul was stressing the significance of this for every person when he wrote to the Christians in Rome, "There is no condemnation for those who are united with Christ Jesus, because in Christ Jesus the life-giving law of the Spirit has set you free from the law of sin and death." (Rom. 8:1-2 NEB.) It takes more than mere adherence to the letter of the law in our behavior. It takes the love of God revealed by him through Jesus Christ. How then do we discover what this all can mean to us in our time, in our particular situation, in our own personal human condition? We need to understand the hold sin has on us, the need for redirecting our lives under God's purpose, and the means available for reconciliation with him and restoration to his fellowship.

Rebellion Against God

Let me remind you that I am well aware that there are some areas of human thought in which sin has been ruled out! The word has been dropped from many vocabularies as an explanation of human behavior, or misbehavior. All I can say is that whatever name you may wish to use, you are referring to the same human experience. You can drop sin from word usage, but the experience which is theologically defined as sin clings closely, dogging our steps each day. Here is the sense of lostness still separating us from the experiences of life which come only in conscious acknowledgment of and fellowship with God. We may be like the guide in the Rocky Mountains who was once asked, "Have you ever been lost in the mountains?" He replied, "No I have never been lost, but once for eight days I was bewildered." Call it what you want, but, when you are victimized by it, the end results are pretty much the same.

There is a cartoon series which features the little monk known as Brother Juniper. In one of the cartoons Brother Juniper is reading the sports page, particularly the box score of a baseball game. This, you will remember, carries the names of all players and lists their personal performance in hits, runs, and errors. Brother Juniper looks up to Brother Sebastian and asks, "How would you like to be in a business that publishes your errors every day?" For most of us that would be devastating.

Let's ask simply what is sin? There are many synonyms for it—estrangement, rebellion, pride, selfishness, self-will, separation—these are all facets of the word and the experience. Basically, we can define sin as an act of rebellion against God; it is any act or attitude that separates us from God. Any act of selfishness is bound to separate us from God. Therefore we identify sin with selfishness.

There is a difference between sin and sins. Sins can be called any particular acts of wrong-doing. Our Roman Catholic friends identify seven of these deadly sins: pride, anger, envy, avarice, sloth, gluttony, lust. These all have in common a violation of Jesus' commandment to love God, self, and neighbor. (Mark 12:30-31.)

Sin, as Georgia Harkness describes it in *What Christians Believe*, is "more persistent and intangible than any particular act of wrongdoing." This happens when sin is the state of the soul. "This roots in our self-will, our indifference to God and His will, our self-righteous attempts to run our own lives in defiance of God and, quite often, in defiance of the feelings and needs of other people." The real question for each of us is simply this: Who can stop sinning of his own will? As Paul puts it, "Miserable creature that I am, who is there to rescue me out of this body doomed to death?" And he answers his own question, "God alone, through Jesus Christ our Lord."

So, if we know what sin is and does and we know that God

82

alone can save us from sin—why then do men sin? The answer appears to be that mistakes seem part and parcel of human existence. Art Linkletter once interviewed a six-year-old youngster and asked her about her favorite Bible story. She replied, "My favorite story is Noah's ark and the flood." Then Mr. Linkletter said, "I want to ask you a question. Noah took all the animals into the ark so that they were saved from the flood, but why did he take into the ark the mosquitoes and the ants?" The little girl thought for a moment and then she replied, "Well, everybody makes some mistakes." You and I are very much among that everybody.

But you are thinking that God could have created us without this yen for sin, without this talent for making not merely one excusable mistake, but a perpetual series of unexcusably repeated mistakes. If he is a good God and loves goodness, why didn't he set up the human situation so there would not be the temptations which prove too strong for us? There is no simple answer. The best answer I know is that God did not choose to create a race of robots. Man is no puppet on a moral string to be controlled by someone upstairs on a platform pulling the strings. God gave us the power of choice within the limitations of space, place, and time. We were made to be morally responsible. Thereby we are free to choose our course of action in given situations. We can exercise this God-given freedom to choose to act irresponsibly and to do evil. Because we are persons with free will, we are able to disobey God and fall into sin by our own choice. And while God alone can save us from our worst selves, his power comes only when we seek that kind of salvation.

Ernest Fremont Tittle once suggested a definition of sin which may have helpfulness for us here, "The best intelligence and the best conscience of this present time unite in saying that sin, fundamentally, is selfishness—the mean decision to secure one's own pleasure, or one's own profit, without any regard to the highest welfare of other people, and without any concern for the purpose of God."

Richard Niebuhr defined sin this way. "All human action, all culture, is infected with godlessness, which is the essence of sin. Godlessness appears as the will to live without God, to ignore him, to be one's own source and beginning, to live without being indebted and forgiven, to be independent and secure in one's self, to be godlike in oneself. It has a thousand forms and expresses itself in the most devious ways. It appears in the complacency of self-righteously moral and of self-authenticatedly rational men, but also in the despair of those for whom all is vanity. It manifests itself in irreligion, in atheism, and anti-theism; but also in the piety of those who consciously carry God around with them wherever they go."

Is there one of us who doesn't find himself reflected in at least one of these characteristics of sinners—and probably in many of them?

Rebirth and Redirection

Methodism has always had much to say about the experience called conversion. This is the experience in which one is re-born to the experience of God and finds his life redirected by the spirit of God's Son. This is in the Wesleyan tradition. The denomination owes its founding to the experience of John Wesley, an Anglican clergyman of the eighteenth century, who became an exemplar of experience-motivated religion. Wesley was in deep torment and dissatisfaction with his own religious life. On May 24, 1738, he went unwillingly to a prayer service in a house in Aldersgate Street in London, not far from St. Paul's Cathedral. He reported on his experience in the following oft-quoted words, "About a quarter before nine, while (he) was describing the change which God works in the heart through faith in Christ, I felt my heart strangely warmed. I felt I did trust in Christ, Christ alone, for salvation; and an assurance was given me that he had taken away my sins, even mine, and saved me from the law of sin and death." Commenting on the fact that we sometimes have misinterpreted Wesley's experience here as his conversion experience, the hour he was saved, Bishop Gerald Ensley points out in *God's Good News,* "Certainly it was not the conversion experience of a bowery mission, a turning from lust or drunkenness or criminality. Wesley was not converted at Aldersgate to the precepts of Christ or from religious indifference. He had been a priest of the Anglican Church for some years when Aldersgate overtook him. In the language of religious psychology, Wesley's experience at Aldersgate was a mystical experience, when the God who had already convinced his mind, and whom he had been trying to serve with his will, at last captured his heart, and all the motivating power of religious feeling poured into him. . . . He was unhappy and without joy in his religious experience. Then came

85

Aldersgate, and he straightened out to live one of the most remarkable lives of his century."

That hits many of us right where we live. We have been
convinced in our minds, we have dedicated our wills, but, perhaps, we have not found the kind of experience of God which
confirms these in our experience. The experience of conversion
means rebirth in the spirit of Christ, redirection of life in the
pattern of his living, after we have been delivered from self-
centered pride. We then find life renewed in the Christian
faith and in Christian practice. George Jackson years ago suggested that "For one man conversion means the slaying of
the beast within him; in another it brings the calm of conviction to an unquiet mind; for a third it is the entrance
into a larger liberty and a more abundant life; and yet again
it is the gathering into one of the forces of a soul at war
within itself."

Among all the definitions of conversion, probably the most
widely accepted is that of Harvard psychologist William
James in *The Varieties of Religious Experience:* "To be converted, to be regenerated, to receive grace, to experience religion, to gain an assurance, are so many phrases which denote
the process, gradual or sudden, by which a self, hitherto
divided, and consciously wrong, inferior and unhappy, becomes unified and consciously right, superior and happy, in
consequence of its firmer hold upon religious realities."

Wallace Hamilton used to put it this way when describing
conversion: "Conversion is that process through which the
redeeming power of God brings all the powers of your being
into perfect focus and coordination—by which He harnesses

the wild horse of your nature to His majestic purposes and makes them the servants of the new life in Christ."

Is there one of us who doesn't desire life to be a unity in which all his powers are focused and coordinated toward happiness and effectiveness in the process of living? Paul assures us that we need not dwell in disunity of personality, unhappiness of soul, and inferiority in feelings. What legalism cannot do, God has done through his spirit in Christ. "There is no condemnation for those who are united with Christ Jeuss, because in Christ Jesus the life-giving law of the Spirit has set you free from the law of sin and death." Such freedom is salvation from sin. And, God alone can give it to us.

Reconciliation and Restoration

Salvation has been called life's truest good. To be saved is life's most cherished desire, whether or not we consciously admit it. Every one of us wants for his life that which is denoted by the terms "being saved" and "salvation." Why? Because, as Nels Ferre points out in *Know Your Faith,* "salvation means getting right with God and that state alone can give man full satisfaction. To be saved means to be right with God, to be in line with His will. Salvation is life's goal because man is God's creature. Salvation is man's main need because God is life's final goal." Salvation requires that we be right with God and that we be right with our fellowmen.

Once we have been convicted of our human sin and found rebirth and redirection through our experience of the religious realities that have come to us from God through Christ, then

87

we are ready for the reconciliation which can take place when we are consciously restored to the household of God's family and rejoin the fellowship of Christian love.

Once again, this all goes back to the basic premise with which we originally began—God can meet our needs, whatever they are, only when we put our ultimate trust in him and in his love. This is basic. This is the threshhold over which we must pass before we can enter into the fellowship of those who have been found in their lostness, saved from their sinful selfishness, and redeemed for God's holy purpose in the human scene. What we have been saying has been said many times before. To quote George Thomas, "To modern man suffering from emptiness of life apart from God, apart from his true or real self, apart from his fellows, there is offered now as in the days of Jesus and Paul, the Christian way of reconciliation to God through Christ. As we have observed earlier, man cannot find peace and joy simply through his 'good works' nor through his social achievements—important and significant to the well-being of the world as these may be. What we need above all else is a faith which will enable us to overcome our fears, our anxieties, our pride, our sensuality, our self-centeredness, our estrangement from God and man, our isolation from the fellowship." Paul and the Christian faith he interprets point out clearly that this can come only through putting our ultimate trust in God and his love. To trust in ourselves will find us continuing in our lostness. To trust in our own man-made value systems leaves us without the dimension of the divine. Trust in God enables us to fill life's emptiness with the joy and peace of his divine will and purpose for our living as his children.

We dare not leave this without acknowledging that, in this age of the absurd, when there is so much acceptance of meaninglessness as the end of life and purposelessness as the end of human existence, there are many specious forms of salvation. We have offered to us various spiritual and political ointments of healing. William Graham Cole discusses these in *The Restless Quest of Modern Man.* "In the theologies of Roman Catholic or Protestant orthodoxy, in the dialectical materialism of Karl Marx (either in its pure form or as revised by Lenin, Stalin, Khrushchev, Kosygin, and Brezhnev and Mao Tse-tung) in the subtleties of Zen Buddhism, in the rationalistic humanism of John Dewey and his disciples, in the existentialist camp of Sartre and Heidegger, or in the psychological insights of psychoanalysis or behaviorism, there are to be found those who feel themselves rescued from the stormy seas of disillusionment. They erect their lighthouses on the rocks of their firm convictions and offer to guide the lost to the safe harbors of the true believer. The problem, however, is that what appears to the faithful adherent as a peaceful mooring seems to the multitude of despisers, both cultured and otherwise, as either a treacherous reef or an empty mirage."

The Christian faith across the centuries has proved an effective means of guiding lives safely into the desired harbor with a minimum of shipwreck on the reefs that may surround it. Christians have known a kind of freedom that is available through no other source than through the God revealed in

89

Jesus. By and through this Jesus of Nazareth we are saved from the death by sin or the sin of living death into fellowship with God. How to prove it? We cannot by mathematical formula or scientific findings. How to know it? We can as we see others whose lives have been changed for the better through their faith in God's love. And we can experience it for ourselves when we can trust God as the power who saves.

These pages are being written in the lakeside study of our family cottage on Lake Michigan. I just returned from a walk up the Epworth Heights beach. I passed the cottage which Bishop William A. Quayle built and occupied. The dormer study where he wrote his books on God and nature forms a modest room where this religious naturalist spent many an hour of creative thought and writing. As a fellow Kansan I met the Bishop only once, when as a youngster I was roller-skating across the campus in Baldwin where he had retired. But his spirit has pervaded that of any preacher who has read his books.

Merton S. Rice relates in his biography how Bishop Quayle was converted as a schoolboy at a revival meeting held in a country schoolhouse in Kansas. He told of that experience in these words, "The preacher came to me and said, 'Billy, you belong to Jesus.' He was a kind of farmer fellow, and he grew all crops but hair, and he wore farmer clothes, and he spoke about farming and sowing, and he said there was a great harvest; and everybody paid heed.

"And then he came and put his hand on my shoulder, and said, 'Billy, God wants you to be one of his farmers.' And I came up the aisle of the school house . . . not to a chancel, there wasn't any. There wasn't anything but a dictionary in the school house, so I came up and bowed at the dictionary; and oh me, the wind was wild that night. It was as stormy as on the wide sea; the storm that beat on the prairie school house, blew like it did on the Sea of Galilee; and Christ came over and said to me, 'Boy, what do you want down here?' And I said, "I want thee, O Christ.' And He said, 'I have come.' "

Now that may sound too sentimental in our sophisticated day. But not to any of the throngs who heard the "Skylark of Methodism" with his spellbinding oratory. Not to any who are a part of the Quayle admirers' cult. For we know what happened as a result of an orphan farm boy whose life was changed that night because God saves.

By whatever process it may happen, salvation brings assurance that God has set us free from the law of sin and death.

God Restores—Reconciliation

Tennessee Ernie Ford came to national prominence singing a modified folk song of the miners called "Sixteen Ton." It bemoaned the plight of the miner who moved "sixteen ton" of rock in the mines in order to keep body and soul together, but found he was always in debt to the company store. He could never avoid getting deeper in debt because, as the refrain suggests, "I owe my soul to the company store." This is certainly not an authentic Christian word. We believe that God has provided for man's salvation and man owes his soul not to man, not to any self-achievement of men, but to God alone.

God's divine purpose for us is that we shall be reconciled to him. His purpose is to reconcile men to himself and to one another in Jesus Christ his Son. Webster defines reconciliation as bringing back to harmony again. If you have heard a piano tuner work, you heard him working with one key and string until it is where his ear tells him it should be in pitch. Then he strikes a chord to see if it is in harmony with the other tuned strings. Is this not in part the picture of what happens when God redeems prodigal man and brings him back into divine harmony? We have heard the experience of conversion spoken of as "getting right with God." And there is much of truth in the comment, from the standpoint of reconciliation.

Alan Richardson speaks of reconciliation as "being readmitted to the presence and favor of our rightful Sovereign after we have rebelled against him." He points out the difference in thought here between the Old and the New Testament. In the former there is the thought that man can atone for himself and his sins by himself and the price he personally pays. But, the New Testament affirms, "God has reconciled rebellious man, who was unable by anything that he could do to establish 'peace' or a right relationship with God."

Paul wrote the Corinthian church about this dynamic quality of the Christian faith. He spoke of the kind of reconciliation which God desires, not the sacrifice of animals, not the many acts of legalistic penance for sin, but the repentance and belief of the person in God's love and his desire to be at one with man. Said Paul, "God was in Christ reconciling the world to himself, not counting their trespasses against them, and entrusting to us the message of reconciliation."

Man's Estrangement

We need to see Jesus' task was not that of reconciling God to man. God needs no such reconciliation. It is man who needs reconciling to God. And this, God was in Christ to accomplish.

Jesus helped us understand what this means in his parable of the Prodigal Son. The father did not encourage the boy to leave home. He wanted him to stay on and be the traditional faithful son of the Hebrew home. But the boy was self-willed and self-centered. He wanted what he wanted and none could tell him how to run his life. So he left. The results were disastrous—he ended up in a pigpen. And there the record says "he came to himself." He saw what he had been, what he had become through his selfishness. He was despondent in his hunger and homesickness for his father's house. When he returned, he found the father waiting to restore him to proper station—the ring, the shoes, the fatted calf—all these had been awaiting his return from estrangement. And what parent cannot understand the father's action here in welcoming back his errant son? The father needed no prodding to be reconciled to the son. But he could not accomplish it alone. Unless and until the son turned from the far country, there could be no reconciliation.

Do not we see in the prodigal son the symbol of our own errant humanity? Self-willed and self-centered, we march away from the Father's house in spiritual estrangement? Note how this estrangement finds expression in ancient and modern man. Harris Franklin Rall summarizes it in these words in *Religion as Salvation:* "Salvation is through union with God. Sin divides. It is more than a matter of debts to be paid or deeds demanding punishment. It is the wrong spirit and life in man, the mighty and destructive power which we see at work in the world today. Ignorance, indifference, folly, selfishness, greed, lust, blindness, and unbelief—sin is all this and more. Reconciliation is always of two. Man has to be brought to see God in his holiness and love, to see himself in his sin and need, to see the new life that was offered him, to give himself utterly in the radical revolution that was demanded."

Man's estrangement from God is expressed in indifference which makes him unaware of God. For such a person God is but a void. He moves through life unaware of the undertow that threatens him, even as he is unaware of the voice of God that calls to him to come back into the harbor. It is reported that one can go boating on the Niagara River above the falls and be unaware that the relatively peaceful river will soon churn into turbulence. Indeed, the point of no return is not always evident to the inexperienced boatman and he could well go beyond it before he is aware of what has happened. Then, unless there is outside rescue, there is little chance that he can avoid being swept over the rapids to almost certain death below. When he becomes aware of his plight, then he may cry out for help and solicit any aid available. So with the person who is indifferent to God—he also is indifferent to human sin. He is just plain unaware that there is any need for reconciliation. But his very indifference is the reason for his estrangement from God.

For another thing, we are estranged from God if we allow any unresolved resentment to rancor within our minds or hearts. Obviously one cannot be reconciled to his former friends so long as he harbors the resentment that may have been responsible for his estrangement from them. Similarly, one cannot be reconciled to God if he harbors resentment toward God for what he feels to be injustice or discrimination. How many of us ask the question, "If God is good, then why does he permit me to suffer in this way, or to fail as I have, or to lose out in competition with others who prove to be more successful in their work than I?"

Certainly we can know what resentment costs us when we fan its flames against our fellows without seeking to smother it. Only the grace of God is sufficient to enable us to overcome this attitude and the actions which result from it. Roland Hayes has been one of the truly great concert singers of our time. He has been an admired friend of mine for more than twenty years. I know, personally, of his sweet spirit, his gracious manner, and his understanding heart. A reporter came to interview him one time before a concert and found him eating his supper in a dingy hotel room because the hotel denied him a better place in which to dine. The reporter, a white man, exploded in anger about this treatment of the great Negro singer, but Mr. Hayes said to him, "My earliest teacher in voice, himself a Negro, told me that as an artist, a black artist, I would suffer terribly if I allowed

96

the barbs to penetrate my soul; but if my heart was right, and my spirit divinely disciplined, then nobody in all the world would be able to hurt me. I know now this is true. I try every moment of every day to live in such awareness of the divine that no bitterness can creep into my heart. Thus I have learned how to be happy, and I have discovered that nobody in all the world can hurt me except myself." [1]

If you have not discovered this spirit, then there may be unresolved resentments in your heart which keep you estranged from God.

Defiant selfishness is the cause of estrangement for many of us. We demand that the world pay attention to us and keep us at the center of the world. And when someone doesn't respond in this fashion then we dismiss him from our self-centered circle. The only way we can return to that circle of fellowship that includes him is to overcome our self-centeredness. This kind of selfishness expresses itself in various ways. There is the self-complacency of the person who feels no need to overcome the gulf between himself and God. He separates himself from God through his self-pity: "I've never had it so tough, and neither has anyone else." Another form of this is the self-righteousness of the person who is always sticking in his thumb and pulling out the plum which prompts him to say constantly, "See what a good boy am I." Do you see that these are forms of selfishness that defy God and keep one apart from him?

A sense of guilt can prevent reconciliation. Sin is any act

---

[1] *Notable Sermons from Protestant Pulpits,* ed. Charles L. Wallis (Nashville: Abingdon Press, 1960), p. 18.

of rebellion against the will of the holy love of God, it is disloyalty toward the Author of Life. Yet, we can become so bogged down in our sins that we feel we have moved beyond the possibilities of redemption. "There is no chance that God could love the likes of me." Plagued by this sense of guilt, we refuse to pick ourselves up out of our pigpen and make the long pilgrimage home to the Father. "How can I face him? How can I look him in the eye and say I am sorry for all this I have done?" Thus spoke a wayward son about the suggestion he return home to his father. Yet, his pastor to whom he said it, knew that the father awaited his return with eagerness to heal the breach between them, to effect reconciliation. The only way was to resolve the overwhelming sense of guilt—and love alone is equal to that. God in his mercy and love has provided for man's reconciliation and return from the land of estrangement.

Disobedient rebellion separates us from God. While an indulgent father let the boy have his way, the prodigal son in Jesus' parable was acting in a way that defiantly was in disobedience to the spirit of his father and the family life he had known. He was in rebellion against it all and went to the far country to escape it. It was in the physical separation that he discovered the spiritual separation which had arisen. It was the thought of this kind of reconciliation and restoration that brought him out of the pigpen and hurried him back toward home. His was a normal teenager's revolt against adult authority and parental domination, carried to the extreme, to be sure. But, if every teenager could know and every parent remember that there is something in the human heart that forces us to explode against the disciplines of home and family and community, which for the first dozen years of our lives we were willing to accept but now find as hampering restraints, then the inevitable estrangement which comes between parents and teen-agers would not be so severe and certainly would not last so long.

Similarly there are those times when we seek our own way rather than God's way. Or we experience those times when we seek to bend God's will to fit our wills rather than seek to obey his divine will. This is the disobedient rebellion which drives a wedge of separation between what God wants for us and what we at the moment are certain we want for ourselves. If you are in that situation, then you are among those who need reconciliation. Few of us are outside this group.

God's Initiative

God is the reconciler and in his "merciful initiative" he has provided for the restoration of prodigal man to the Father's house. Summarizing the history of God's action toward his children in providing for their redemption from sin, their reconciliation and atonement with him, Joseph Haroutunian says: "The whole history of redemption from Abraham to our own day could well be understood as God's effort to reconcile man to himself, to God, and to his neighbor. To this end was the exodus and the covenant, the Law and the prophets, and the whole controversy of God with His people, culminating in Him who lived and died in freedom from man's universal subjection to the power of death, sin, the devil, and the world. Jesus Christ thus became the possibility created by 'the living God' for a restoration of man to sanity and wholeness as 'intelligent creation,' and the possibility of freedom from the domination of death. Thus, God's justice, which is the law of man's existence as creature was satisfied, man's sin covered, man's spirit purified, and the condition of man's love for man as creature, without which there can be no human fruition, fulfilled. And this is what we might today understand by the atonement." [2]

In this action God has not only removed the guilt or penalty of sin, but has brought about a restored personal relationship and fellowship with man. Paul made it clear that the process of reconciliation involved this, for he saw God as "not counting their trespasses against them." But we need, with Dietrich Bonhoeffer, to recognize that there is such a thing as "cheap grace." By that he meant that we assume that there is no price tag attached at our end of the line. Because God is a loving heavenly Father, we may assume he is merely a genial benevolent grandfather who will wink at wickedness so long as we turn aside on occasion and pay our respects to our elders. But one cannot see and accept God's mercy without his justice. We cannot receive his love without his righteousness. However, when one is truly penitent and humble, when he returns from the far country of indifference or indulgence or resentment and acknowledges his sin and asks for restoration, then the process of reconciliation

[2] *A Handbook of Christian Theology,* ed. M. A. Halverson (Meridian books, Cleveland: World, 1959), p. 21.

is underway. And he will find his sins have been redeemed and he is at one with God.

In Christ the God of love was joined to man in a life of love. Bishop Angus Dun in his Yale Lectures on preaching said, "Jesus was sent to restore men to wholeness by renewing their relationship with that Other who is the very ground of their being, sent by the Father—Believing imagination has seen in the Saving Person a rescuer, coming to men isolated by sin from God, from their fellows as ultimately brothers in God, from themselves as ultimately sons of God." It is God's initiative in providing for our redemption. None can wander completely outside the circle of his divine forgiving love. God seeks them out wherever they are and awaits their willingness to be restored to the family circle again. "God was in Christ"—actively engaged in a divine and loving ministry of reconciliation. In the words of the hymn,

> I sought the Lord, and afterward I knew
> He moved my soul to seek him, seeking me;
> It was not I that found, O Saviour true,
> No, I was found of thee.
> I find, I walk, I love, but oh, the whole
> Of love is but my answer, Lord to thee!
> For thou wert long beforehand with my soul;
> Always thou lovedst me.

Man's Restored Relationship

Basically, let it be said that reconciliation means restored personal fellowship. This is true on the level of human rela-

101

tionship and on the level of our relationship with God. One sees man's need for this kind of personal fellowship in the Broadway musical of a number of years ago, *Plain and Fancy*. The story took place in an Amish community in Pennsylvania. The plot was centered about the Amish custom of punishing a person for wrong-doing; they call the punishment "shunning." The condemned person continues to live in family and community, but no one in the family or outside is permitted to speak to the person or to act as if he even exists. There is a severe penalty attached to anyone who breaks the regulation on shunning. As one observed the action on stage, he found himself sympathetically identifying with the person being shunned by family and friends. We could see why this discipline is a good deterrent to any person who is tempted to deviate from the pattern and the procedures of that exclusive community. The day of restoration when the sentence of shunning was at an end for this person was a joyous occasion, not only for the suffering culprit whose crime or failure had resulted in the estrangement from the fellowship, but also for his family and friends. He was restored to the community. He was brought back from the far country of his separation—though he had never left home in a physical or geographical sense.

This is an accurate picture of many of our lives which are lived apart from God. God does not impose the "shunning" on us except that he has established certain bases on which we can enjoy personal fellowship with him. When we violate the spirit of that fellowship, when we sin in ways that set us apart from God, then we are in need of being reconciled, of being brought again into the fellowship.

Reconciliation, says Alan Richardson, is "being readmitted to the presence and favor of our rightful Sovereign after we have rebelled against him." And this is an act of God to which we need only make honest and conscious response.

Reconciliation means you know you are accepted. Paul Tillich has helped us at this point when he suggested that the big step for anyone of us in our relationship with God is to realize that God accepts us even when we are unacceptable, even when man will not accept us, and even when we will not accept ourselves as worthy of fellowship. God loves you, God cares for you, God accepts you—even when you declare that God is dead. Reconciliation for the prodigal son in Jesus' parable came finally when he found his father accepted him because he loved him. He learned to his surprise that he had never been unaccepted of his father. His father was ready any day or night to receive him back into the circle of personal fellowship. The boy had to come to himself in a pig sty before he was led to learn the fact of his acceptance by his father. This happens to many of us who wander in some far country apart from God in our loneliness and tragic sorrow. Once we learn the fact that God has accepted us and that reconciliation depends only on our willingness to return to our Father's House, then most of us are ready to hasten toward that cherished reunion with a loving Father.

Reconciliation means God who loves and accepts us, forgives and forgets. He will not remember your sins against you, said Jesus, when you penitently come before his presence to seek forgiveness. This is not easy for us to understand because it is never easy for us to forgive and forget. We can better understand the wife, who blurted out to the marriage counsellor as she and her wayward husband were seeking to patch up the pieces of a marriage that was disintegrating, "I am willing to forgive and forget. But I can't promise to forget that I have forgiven and forgotten." Not so our God. Jesus promised that God removes our guilt when in obedience and love we return to his house from our wandering in the far country. The father did not bargain with the prodigal son. He did not suggest that they negotiate their differences and find out where in his retinue of servants he could place the returning prodigal. The father rushed out, put the ring of sonship on his finger, the robe of freedom on his shoulders, and the shoes that symbolized he was no longer a servant on his bare feet. Here was a real case of resurrection. "He that was lost is found, he that was dead is alive again." This is reconciliation for any man.

We are reconciled through God's overwhelming love as expressed on the cross. Here is revealed the tender heart of a God of eternal loving-kindness. Who is there who can stand long in the shadow of the cross without growing taller in his spiritual stature? For some years I served a downtown church in Jackson, Michigan. We built a new chapel with an entrance directly from the busy main street. As we talked about its design, someone suggested that he hoped it would be so arranged that a passerby looking in could see the cross on the altar. And so indeed, it was. As you pass by the open doors of the chapel, your attention is immediately drawn up the aisle to the cross on the altar. For every Christian of any sensitivity, this can be an experience of remembering, even for a moment, the irresistible love of God which overwhelms us and prompts us to cry out for reconciliation and redemption from the habits and attitudes that have separated us from that divine love.

The Reconciled Are Reconcilers

We miss the mark if we think of this business of being reconciled to God as purely something that happens to us. When it does happen to us, God and men can assume something will happen through us. As Paul put it "All this is from God, who through Christ reconciled us to himself and gave us the ministry of reconciliation—entrusting to us the message of reconciliation." The reconciled must reconciler be.

For most of us this may not prove as costly as it did for Jesus. Yet, there have been many martyrs in the past and the present who have given the "last full measure of devotion" in the witness to Christian reconciliation. In T. S. Eliot's *Murder in the Cathedral,* he includes in the archbishop's Christmas sermon these words: "A martyr, a saint, is always made by the design of God, for His love of men, to warn them and to lead them, to bring them back to His ways. A martyrdom is never the design of man; for the true martyr is he who has become the instrument of God, who has lost his will in the will of God . . . . (he) no longer desires anything for himself, not even the glory of martyrdom."

This spirit is found in many lives today, who, having

known the reconciling love of God, feel called to become agents of reconciliation. They risk life and limb, reputation and future to make constructive efforts for peace and unity.

William Stringfellow is an Episcopal layman who has invested his life in living and working with racial problems in Harlem. In a recent book he tells of an incident, out of which the plot for *West Side Story* came. The Puerto Rican boys and the Italian boys in the area were fighting over the right to swim in a public pool. With knives and chains and bottles they engaged in brutal warfare.

In every gang there is a war counsellor. He is not the gang's leader. He is the cleverest boy and his job is to chart the activity of the gang—where they will rob, whom they will fight, how they will do it. The brother of the war counsellor for the Italian gang was killed. The counsellor brooded all night afterward planning how the gang would get its revenge. He loved his brother very much. But suddenly there came the realization that if they got revenge, it would be somebody else's brother who would be killed.

Early the next morning, he went alone without weapons, and unknown to any of his gang, to seek out the war counsellor of the rival gang which had killed his brother. He wanted to know if there was some way their gang warfare could be stopped without more killing or without either of the gangs losing face. So instead of plotting against each other, the two boys worked out a plan of peace and reconciliation.

Mr. Stringfellow says that this act of courage on the part of the Italian boy saved the day. If he had failed he probably would have been killed by his own gang. But because of what he did peace came to that section of East Harlem. The two gangs compromised their differences and the city was given an opportunity to help the boys. This one boy's effort at reconciliation meant a whole new horizon of hope and opportunity rather than continued struggle and death for the neighborhood boys in East Harlem. He paid the cost of being reconciled. The reconciled of God must reconciler be.

God Redeems—Atonement

On the campus of the University of Chicago stands the Ricketts Memorial Laboratory. An inscription explains the memorial: "In Memory of Howard Taylor Ricketts, assistant professor of pathology, whose life, already marked by rare achievement in medical research, was cut short by an epidemic of typhus fever which he was studying in Mexico City." In these few words is the dramatically simple story of sacrifice and courage. This brilliant young student and teacher of another generation, who had already conquered spotted fever, plunged into an epidemic of typhus fever. He suspected that as the wood tick carried the germ of spotted fever, so the body louse carried the germ of typhus. Seeking to find the bacillus, he, with an assistant, examined hundreds of insects and blood cultures. They found the organism and the fight with the disease was won. His research literally saved Europe from an epidemic of typhus fever. When the disease broke out in Serbia during World War I, it was the results of Ricketts' study which stopped it. Though the Chicago scientist conquered the disease, he himself lost his life. One of the insects he was studying bit him and he died from the disease from which he was to save thousands of others.

We can thrill to such a story of heroism and sacrifice. And we can understand why many others have done the same thing in their area of medical research. Given such opportunity and ability, few persons would back down from the sense of duty and obligation which these impose.

The New Testament is the story of how Christ brought salvation to mankind, even though it cost him his life. Paul was trying to explain this sacrifice to the Roman Christians and said, "Yet the proof of God's amazing love is this: That is was while we were sinners that Christ died for us" (Rom. 5:8 Phillips).

Many persons who can understand stories of sacrifice and heroism among their fellows stumble when they seek to understand the sacrificial death of Jesus on the cross. Atonement, sacrifice, cross, reconciliation, forgiveness of sins, redemption —these are oft-used words in our religious language. But how much do we really understand of what we are saying in these words?

It is not always easy to translate into understandable language for the man in the pew what these theological terms mean for him. They have often become overlaid with a variety of interpretations. Thus they may well lose the basic contribution they could make to our knowledge of God and his love for us.

In brief, atonement is the restoration of man to a right relationship with God through the obedience, sacrificial love and death of Jesus Christ. The late Joseph Hartounian summarized the various interpretations in these words: "Beyond this, the doctrine of the atonement is as many-sided as man's alienation from God and the aspects of the 'work of Christ' which corresponds to it. As sin against God has been thought of in terms of disobedience to the Law, a criminal act, a corruption, an alienation, a bondage; so, correspondingly, the atonement has been thought of in terms of the satisfaction of God's justice (Anselm), the expiation of crime by punishment (Calvin), a cleansing or purification especially by the self-sacrifice of Christ, a reconciliation, and a victory over the devil and deliverance from the thralldom of evil powers such as sin, the law, death, wrath and the world (Luther)."

It may help us, in our search for an understanding of how God meets our needs, to listen to what the New Testament says, what Jesus said, and what men today say about the atonement, and then to see what it says to us in our life today.

What Does the New Testament Say?

One day my daughter was sitting in my parsonage study looking at a book of religious art. This was occupying her attention as a four-year-old while I sat at my desk in the effort to study. I was suddenly aroused from my reveries by her startling question. She showed me a picture of the crucifixion and asked, "Why have they got Jesus up on that board?" That states a question that concerns far more of us than a four-year-old youngster! Haven't you asked yourself that question at times? The New Testament was written in an effort to put that question in its proper context and provide us a reasonable and acceptable answer.

The writers of the gospels and the epistles were trying to explain to a world which knew nothing about Jesus whom they called Christ, what the death of Jesus really means. One can quickly sense the severe difficulties under which they labored in this effort. Their Messiah had been done to death as a common criminal. They had held some grandiose hopes for what the fulfillment of the Messianic kingdom would mean for them. The cross had shattered those dreams. But it was followed immediately by the Resurrection. This changed the entire picture—both of what they could properly expect of God's Messiah and of the revival of their hope for the Kingdom. Yet, consider how impossible the task. How could they explain why One who is God Incarnate with divine power to command legions of angels, would allow himself to be crucified? Either he was powerless to prevent it and was thus a counterfeit Christ, or he represented a God who might have, but didn't, intercede to prevent this apparent destruction of the dream.

The death of Christ is central in any consideration of his life, his work, and his mission. But we need to see that it is not a separate act nor an isolated item in the life experience on earth of one, Jesus of Nazareth. You cannot isolate Calvary from

Bethlehem. You cannot look at Golgotha without looking also at the empty tomb. You cannot understand the crucifixion apart from the Incarnation. So, the New Testament writers put them all in the context of the life and death and resurrection of their leader. And we must catch this gospel perspective if we are to understand at all the death of Jesus and what it means for our personal salvation and that of our world. As Dean Austin Farrar puts it in *A Faith of Our Own:* "It (the cross) was one action, one sacrifice, by which Christ saved us; the Bible, and especially St. Paul, holds that unity fast, but dwells now on one aspect of it, now on another. If we consider how utterly undeserved it was, we call it grace; if we consider the cost, we call it atonement; if we consider the effect we call it new life, redemption, sanctification. . . . God provided in Christ's death the spiritual cure for our sin; that is what St. Paul is saying. Yet the proof of God's amazing love is this: that it was while we were sinners that Christ died for us.' "

Now, it needs to be noted that one does not find authoritative doctrine on the Atonement in the New Testament. Harris Franklin Rall suggests that the use of analogies and symbols from the Old Testament and from the traditional Jewish faith and common life is but an effort to answer the basic question of Jesus' death in the context of the Judaistic concept of sacrifice. The gospel writers used the sacrificial system of the Old Testament to explain the function of Jesus in his death. The author of the Epistle to the Hebrews likens him to the High Priest of Israel who made sacrifice for the people. This had been called for in the Mosaic Covenant during Israel's wandering in the desert. Similarly, he writes, sacrifice was required for the establishment of the New Covenant in Christ.

Other New Testament writers found in the penal concept of Jewish faith an explanation for the death of Jesus. Jesus took the judgment on himself for the sins of the new Israel. He went to his death because of man's sin; Jesus accepted for himself the penalty of human sinfulness. Still others of the writers refer to the idea of the cancellation of debts through the payment of the life of Jesus. This is a symbol out of civil law. One finds himself in debt and unable of his own resources to pay. Someone else steps up to the bench and pays the debt and the penalty. Then the debtor, without having paid anything himself, is freed from that debt. Charles Wesley expressed this idea when he wished for a thousand tongues in order to be able to sing the praise due our Redeemer, because:

> He breaks the power of cancelled sin,
>   He sets the prisoner free;
> His blood can make the foulest clean;
>   His blood availed for me.

We need very quickly to see, however, that the New Testament writers, whatever their interpretation of the cross, saw it together with the manger and the tomb. We have only a distorted picture if we fail to see the Atonement and the Incarnation within the same frame as the Resurrection. When we see them together, we grasp more fully the idea that God was incarnate in Jesus Christ, that God so loved the world he gave his Son, and that Son gave himself in sacrificial love for the sins of all mankind. With this perspective we are enabled to understand that this is God's way of coming to man for man's redemption. The cross is the place where the love of God and the life of man are bound together into one. So we call the process *at-one-ment*.

What Did Jesus Say?

If we can accept the "work of Christ" as bringing man and God into at-one-ment, then we need to see how Jesus conceived of his work. He entered the ministry with the conviction that God had called him to proclaim the coming of the Kingdom of Heaven. He echoed here the words of John the Baptist. John was the forerunner, the herald who announced the coming of God's Messiah. He pointed to Jesus as the one who had been sent to bring fulfillment to the hopes of Israel. Here was God's anointed. (See Matt. 3:1-7; Mark 1:4-11.) I believe it was at the time of his baptism by John, that Jesus became aware of the unique role he was to play in the plan of God for the salvation of his people. He confirmed these feelings during the days of spiritual struggle in the wilderness following his baptism. So, whatever Jesus may have said concerning his work must be seen against this kind of background in his acceptance of a divine call and his sense of divine mission.

Jesus considered his task to be one, first of all, of witness to the revelation of God's love and proclamation of that love made available to mankind. So he brought that witness in his ministry of preaching and teaching and healing. He proclaimed the need for repentance that one might prepare himself for the Kingdom citizenship. But soon he discovered that man was not ready to accept God's love simply through the spoken witness of his messenger. Across Jesus' path there loomed through all his ministerial days the shadow of the cross.

Jesus early saw that if he were sincerely to follow God's will for his life without stint or compromise, he could not complete his witness short of the cross. He must give his life in death if man was to have the life that conquers death. Here was no fatalistic following of a predestined path, going as "a quarry slave scourged to his dungeon." Rather here was purposeful acceptance of the role of Christian witness, with the frank recognition that inevitably the cross stood at the end of such a path. Thus, Jesus identified himself with the suffering servant about whom we read in Isaiah 53. He had no illusions that he was a second King David who would restore the military might of ancient Israel. One does not save the souls of people in this majestic fashion, though he may give them a better place in the sun of his day. Thus Jesus was day by day "steadfastly setting his face to go to Jerusalem."

"The death of Jesus must be thought of in close relation to what came before and after it," writes Georgia Harkness in *What Christians Believe.* "In this total ministry God was speaking through his Son and drawing men away from sin to salvation. In Jesus' obedience even to death and in the resurrection which followed, God's love and mercy and God's power over sin and death become unmistakably clear."

Harris Franklin Rall reminded us that the cross for Jesus was first a final witness to the mission he felt called to carry out, and a final appeal to people who had rejected the mission of his message and ministry. Here was an effort dramatically to

115

describe the kind of love God has for man. Albert C. Knudson writes in *The Doctrine of Redemption* that the cross is for us a symbol of "a God of infinite power who solely because of His love, suffers for men and with them."

Moreover, here in the cross was Jesus' final act of obedience to God. One who lived each day in accordance with a will that was identified with the Father's will, now comes to the final demand—the cross. He could have escaped; he could have compromised the situation and pointed out that at thirty-three he had a good twenty to thirty years of preaching and witness left. But the Garden prayers brought the assurance that there was no other way but the cross. And here is the symbol of his final and complete obedience to the divine will for one who would be the Savior of mankind.

Here also, the cross for Jesus becomes the final act of sacrificial love. Here is the divine love of God expressed in this extreme fashion. Thus, Paul can later say to the Romans that this kind of sacrificial love should be studied and understood by men. "Yet the proof of God's amazing love is this: that it was while we were sinners that Christ died for us."

What Do Men Say?

In any of the theological doctrines of the Christian church you will find many shades of disagreement. It looks different to everyone. Each expression of doctrine is subject to personal interpretation. It is like an artist who was irate at an art gallery which had put his work on exhibition. They had hung a picture upside down. As soon as his temper cooled down and the official could explain, the artist was not so mad. It seems the price had been set at $19. And the picture had sold readily in its upside-down state. But the price tag was upside down too —so the artist realized $61 rather than $19.

Many persons speak glibly of the particular theory of the Atonement they may champion. Yet, often, they fail to realize that the atonement as a doctrine was not formulated for 150 to 200 years after Christ. We must remember that these early Christians had the advantage of personal word from those who had known Jesus, or who had known those who knew him. They were, many of them, of Jewish descent and knew of the close relation between Christ and the Old Testament prophecies and of the sacrificial images which had come down from ancient Judaism. The constant threat of their own suffering and death as Christians left no room for the temptation to believe that they could conquer in their own strength (as many today would feel) and still follow Christ to the arena.

The demand for doctrine soon came with questions from outsiders who would ask, "Why should we believe in Jesus?" The individual then needed to be challenged with the historic facts of the gospel. Herein came the need for a theory as to the Atonement for an explanation of why Jesus went to the cross.[1]

The early church fathers, such as Irenaeus, Origen, Athanasius, and Augustine, explained it on the basis of a ransom theory. This simply stated as fact that God had paid

[1] See this historically traced in Robert S. Paul, *The Atonement and the Sacraments* (Nashville: Abingdon Press, 1960), pp. 35-64.

a ransom to the devil to buy men back from the slavery of sin. Christ was the price of the ransom he paid. Thus were the captive slaves redeemed. Implicit in this theory also was the idea that Christ was the victim of death and the devil. But he also was the victor over death and evil in the Resurrection.

Anselm, the twelfth-century Archbishop of Canterbury, stated what is called the satisfaction theory of the Atonement. "He taught that Christ paid for us our debt to God's offended majesty, as if sin were a kind of debt which could be paid off for us, that the sacrifice of Christ sufficed for the debt of all mankind, but would in fact avail to save only enough persons to make up the number of fallen angels." [2]

There are other forms of this "substitutionary" theory of atonement. All of them point to the fact that Jesus has taken man's place and has given his life for man's redemption. Most such theories involve ransom or payment or reparations to the devil or to an offended God—Jesus makes the payment through his life for our sins.

Peter Abelard authored a theory known as the moral influence theory. This was picked up by Horace Bushnell and others who rebelled against the picture which the other theories gave us of God as an inexorable, feudal kind of patriarch who had to be appeased or satisfied. Abelard's theory found in the example of Christ sufficient spiritual shock to bring a person to recognize what God's love is and means to him, because now "God is in Christ more fully bound to man by love" and

[2] Nathaniel Micklem, *Ultimate Questions* (Nashville: Abingdon Press, 1955), p. 115.

we in turn will not shrink from any demands of this love upon us.

More recently, the Scandinavian theologian Gustav Aulen, in his *Christus Victor,* advances the idea that the motif in which the Christian faith expresses most profoundly the meaning of the Atonement is that of God's warfare against evil and his winning of the victory through Christ.

And even more recently, William J. Wolf speaks concerning the consensus of ecumenical insight on the Atonement, "For, the work of atonement is, throughout, the expression of God's holy love. It is love that leads the Father to beget the Son, in the fullness of time to be born as a humble man, and to pour out his life in sacrificial self-giving. It is holy love again after his death and resurrection that causes him to send the Holy Spirit to lead men to respond to his saving work for them."

Moreover, one finds further helpful insight in the comments of the Hindu philosopher, S. Radhakrishnan, writing in *East and West In Religion,* "The mystery of life is creative sacrifice. It is the central idea of the Cross, which was such a scandal to the Jews and the Greeks, that he who truly loves us will have to suffer for us, even to the point of death. . . . The Cross signified that evil in the hour of its supreme triumph, suffers its decisive defeat by the force of patient love and suffering."

For me, Bishop Bromley Oxnam's idea in *A Testament of Faith* finds acceptance as I try to interpret for my life the atoning death of Jesus: "Personally I believe the love of God responds to the repentant sinner, and forgiveness does follow. I do not think telling beads or going on pilgrimage or relying upon someone else to pay for me does it. No, it was 'Amazing grace, how sweet the sound!' Yes, He died for me, and for every man, not to pay an angry God but to overwhelm me with irresistible love, showing me the Father's heart and summoning me to the Father's house. He is my Saviour."

What Does the Atonement Say to Us Today?

By now, you may have deserted these pages because you are "up to here" in the theological disputes and theories of interpretations. No more of this historical and theoretical analysis, you say. You want to know just what, if anything, this doctrine has to say to those of us called to live in the complexity of the twentieth century, particularly in these days when all theology, and even the idea of God's existence itself, seems to be "up for grabs." So, what does the idea of the Atonement say to us and do for us in our day?

For one thing, it reminds us that God's love is undefeatable and without limit. Can you think of any greater test of the reality of one's love than the cross? Can you imagine a God who can express his love for us so sacrificially establishing any kind of limit on his love or his forgiveness? The day of the crucifixion of Jesus marked the darkest hour in human history. Yet, as we look at that lonely cross against the darkening sky of Calvary, we see in it the perspective of the brightness of the Easter dawn—the day of Resurrection. This is the symbol of love that triumphs as the cross is the symbol of love that sacrifices. These expressions of God's love and God's power remind us that whatever we may be, we cannot be beyond God's redeeming love and saving power, as written by Whittier:

> I know not where his islands lift
> Their fronded palms in air;
> I only know I cannot drift
> Beyond his love and care.

James Michener puts this need for assurance into the words of Vito, the puppeteer in one of his novels. Vito came to feel "that any life in this world, no matter how tangled or distressed, could be set free if only a friend knew which snarled string to unravel." The Christian faith believes that this friend is to be found in Jesus whose life, death, and resurrection assures us that God has a love without limit, a power beyond defeat, and a knowledge of which snarled string of sinful man to touch in order to set him free.

Moreover, the Atonement shows us how far God goes to make us free. The cross symbolizes that there is no limit to God's love. And also, it shows that there is no limit to the extent God will go in order that we his children may be freed from the curse of evil and sin. This is not to give aid and comfort to those who assume that they can sin more because then grace will abound even more. Nor should this encourage those who assume because God has paid the price they have no price to pay. Jesus' imperative was: Repent and Believe. Unless we accept that word, we cannot enter into the joy of life that is at one with God and with our fellow-men.

Let us repeat in a personal application that forgiveness and redemption depend on the divine initiative of God. My mother loved me from the day of my birth until the day of her death. I believe she loves me still. Certainly not because I qualify for her love in any way, but because it is the maternal initiative to love one's child, however unlovely and unlovable he may be or become. We who are parents ourselves can understand this. Can we understand then, also, the fact of God's divine fatherly initiative in loving his children? If we can gain even a small insight into God's love in this fashion, we are better able to understand the cross as our symbol of divine love and forgiveness and redemption of mankind.

Finally, the Atonement calls us to see the life we have been saved for and saved to through God in Christ. In the Incarnation, God came alive in the human scene, entering the arena of human experience. In the Atonement, God expressed his limitless love for us in that it was even "while we were sinners that Christ died for us," giving his life for our redemption. In these two basic doctrines of the Christian faith we see reflected the kind of life we who love God have been called to live. It is the life of Christ as well as the death of Christ that brings us to eternal life.

"In the days before blood transfusion was in widespread use, a still remarkable operation took place in New York City. A baby girl's life was ebbing away. Drop by drop an internal hemorrhage was sapping her already limited vitality.

The best medical resources could not control the situation. As a last desperate chance, a direct transfusion from the father to the child was tried. The father's arm was laid bare for six inches, and an artery extracted. With infinite patience and care, the surgeon connected it with a vein in the baby's leg. Soon the current of blood was allowed to flow from one to the other. Then followed one of the most dramatic scenes in medical history. The child, waxen white in her depleted blood supply, lay motionless beside her father. To all appearances, she was without life at all. Presently, a faint tinge of pink appeared on the rim of the ear. Then a glow suffused the whole body. The skin became normal, the fingers and toes taking on a rosy hue. Suddenly the lips of the baby opened and she gave a lusty cry. It was the cry of a life renewed.[8]

Here was an instance in which the life of a child was literally purchased with the father's blood. But will you note that it was not the father's suffering which saved his baby daughter—it was his very life itself.

So God in Christ has linked his life with ours. Through our veins pulses the very dynamic quality of the divine. Through Christ we experience at-one-ment. We are at one with God.

[8] William Adams Brown, *Treasury of the Christian Faith* (New York: Association Press, 1949), p. 211.

God Is One—Trinity

So you have trouble trying to figure out how God can be one and yet three, how Father, Son, and Holy Ghost are three persons yet one? If it is any comfort to you, you have legions of fellow wonderers.

There is much more to this, as we shall see, but let me begin with a story which suggests how one person can be many persons. The keeper of the general store in a small village bought a fresh stock of goods from a wholesaler, but neglected to pay for it. He ignored the series of dunning letters which arrived. So the wholesaler wrote to the local bank to check on his customer's credit rating. Then he wrote to the county judge to get the name of the best lawyer in those parts. He even wrote to the station master to make certain the goods had actually been delivered.

Back came this note: "As station master I delivered your goods O.K. As owner of the store I signed receipt for same. As bank president I O.K. my credit. As judge I recommend myself as the best lawyer in these parts. And if I wasn't the pastor too, I'd tell you to go to hell!"

Absurd as it sounds, that story implies that on the human level the same person can be known in various personalities and positions. He can exercise himself in one or another of them independently of the others.

It would be stupid to assume that this is a parallel to the Christian doctrine of the Trinity. I introduce it simply to point out how we can understand such a person of many positions in the human scene. Is it possible to move from the ridiculous to the sublime and see that God can be one Person yet Three?

A recent magazine story tells of a rash of new cultic forms of religion which have sprung up on the west coast. In one of these, which seems to have a real appeal for "hippies," the swami's name is Chin Maya Nander. He teaches about a god named OM. He greets his worshippers with the words "Hari Om." It is translated, "May you have a big share of the Absolute."

Organized religion seeks to do just that for its worshippers —to enable them to share more fully in the God they worship and the life which he ordains them to live in the human scene. Beliefs, doctrines, and practices emerge in every religious group as means toward the end of identifying the human life with the life of God, of bringing constant assurance that there is indeed fellowship between God and man.

125

Thus, we have in our Christian faith the doctrine of the Trinity—an effort to interpret and/or explain the oneness of God who has expressed himself in Father, in Son, and in Holy Spirit.

John Deschner writes in *We Believe,* "The doctrine of the Trinity is the great doctrine of the oneness of God. It is the Christian answer to idolatry. . . . The Christian Gospel teaches us that there is one triune (three-in-one) God, and that He is the conqueror of all other gods." The Trinity is an expression of the fact that we know the love of God the Father through the gift of the Son, Jesus Christ, in the power of the Holy Spirit.

Now this is baffling to many persons, both inside the church and outside. We secretly wonder whether this Father, Son, and Holy Spirit routine we repeat doesn't reflect three gods instead of one. The Jews, our fathers in faith, stoutly held out for monotheism. And we get pretty confused when we try to say we have one God but that he is expressed in three ways, or described in three ways, or that perhaps there is one God who is a Spirit, and Jesus, along with other prophets, teaches men about him. It gets pretty confusing and frustrating to the average man in the pew. And, the man in the street is lost if he gives it even a moment's thought. As theologian Leonard Hodgson put it in the Croal Lectures in *The Doctrine of the Trinity:* "How many Christians today, when trying to speak of the faith by which they live, would select the doctrine of the Trinity as that to whose truth their whole being vibrates? How many laymen would not rather regard it as an unintelligible metaphysical doctrine which orthodoxy requires them to profess, but which has no direct relevance to their life or their prayers? How many clergy, as Trinity Sunday draws near, groan within themselves as the thought that it will be their duty to try to expound this dry and abstract doctrine to congregations for whom they anticipate that it will have but little interest?" To which most of us will say a hearty "Amen!"

Yet, grapple with it we must. That is, if we are to fathom at all what our forefathers in the Christian faith were trying to say through it. And understand the Trinity we should try, even if just to know what it is we are prepared to reject as an unacceptable way to interpret the unity of the God of Jesus.

We need to see, for instance, at the outset, that we are not talking here about a revelation. As Walter Russell Bowie stated it in *Jesus and the Trinity,* "The doctrine of the Trinity thus is not a revelation; it is a derivation. It is what the mind derives as its own most reverent and thoughtful interpretation of the infinite Reality which is directly known only in the actualities of life. Therefore, the doctrine of the Trinity, insofar as it is true to the living revelation in the Incarnate Lord, has the authority of the road sign which says to us, "In this direction is the Way to God"; but no language or name upon the sign can presume to be a final indication of the inner nature of the infinite One to whom it points."

While there are some few New Testament references which gather up the terms "Father, Son, and Holy Spirit," the Trinity is not a biblical doctrine as such. One can imply some meanings from the brief references to it. One such text is

127

from Paul's final benediction in the second Corinthian letter. Paul offered this blessing, "The grace of the Lord Jesus Christ, and the love of God, and the fellowship of the Holy Spirit, be with you all." (2 Cor. 13:14, NEB) And you have heard that benediction given at the close of many a service of Christian worship whatever the denomination and wherever you were in the world.

We need to see the doctrine in its proper historical perspective. *The Interpreter's Bible* states: "This verse is not a formal statement of the doctrine of the Trinity, but it reflects the aspects of divine redemption and Christian experience which led the church later to formulate this doctrine as the best expression it could give to the Christian understanding of God."

How the Doctrine Came to Be

We need to realize that the doctrine of the Trinity which held that there is a triune nature of God came out of the religious experience of the early Christian community. In its own experience the early church came to know God in three ways. They shared the faith of Judaism in the God of the Old Testament, the Creator God who was in covenant with his people from the days of Abraham and Moses on down to John the Baptist. Then Jesus of Nazareth had come into the world to challenge men and claim them for discipleship with a New Covenant with this same God of Abraham, Isaac, and Jacob. The Christians experienced God as redemptively present in Jesus Christ as Saviour and Lord. After Jesus' departure from the disciples, they no longer saw him in physical form. Yet, they experienced a continuing sense of his abiding presence in their fellowship and in their lives. They knew the reality of the Christ-like presence of God bringing forgiveness and power, and effecting moral transformation in their personal lives and in their fellowship as Christians. Knowing God in these three differing but dovetailing ways, the Christians expressed this in these words of the Pauline benediction—Father, Son, and Holy Spirit.

This created a problem for them. Lycurgus M. Starkey, Jr. phrases the problem in *The Work of the Holy Spirit:* "How were they to explain this experience of knowing God in three ways? How were they to hold to their Jewish inheritance of monotheism and yet give honest expression to their conviction that Jesus was divine?" After many attempts to solve the doctrinal problem by compromising the testimony of experience, the church at Nicaea, in A.D. 325, formulated a definition of this experience into what we know as the doctrine of the Trinity.

We cannot fully understand the implications of the doctrine unless we know something of the specific problems which gave rise to the Council of Nicaea and to subsequent councils, which gave attention to the minutiae of expressing the common beliefs of the Christian faith. Nicaea dealt with the problems growing out of how Christians could and should interpret God and Jesus. For instance, a man named Arius, as described in the *Layman's Guide to Protestant Theology,* put forward the theory that Christ was really a lesser god created by God. "This lesser god came to earth in the man Jesus who was not really a man at all, but a divine being freed from the normal limitations of humanity." Now, if the Arian group could have carried the day for their interpretation, they would have made Jesus less than God, although more than man. This could mean only that Christianity would have moved back to the stage of paganism where it would have had many gods. Jesus of Nazareth would be neither God nor man. Moreover, it would have left God as apart from man, uninterested in his salvation and unapproachable by any of the human race. One can assume that this could well have relegated Christianity to being just another of the pagan mystery religions which abounded in those days in that part of the world.

Another heretical group was known as the Gnostics. While there were many differing expressions of this belief, all Gnostics took their stance in denying that Jesus was in any sense a true human being. You see, this did not deny that Jesus was divine—it just denied that Jesus was human. Since the basis of the Christian faith is rooted in the revelation of God in Jesus Christ through his Incarnation—his coming into the life of humanity—the doctrine of the humanity of Jesus is essential to any Christian understanding of God. It is through Jesus Christ we know the nature of God, his reality as a person. It is through Jesus Christ we feel God's power for salvation and moral direction. In Jesus Christ we feel God's presence and are guided by his wisdom and sustained by his strength. Theoretically, all this could happen if Jesus were only divine and not human. But actually, the heart of the Christian gospel would be destroyed if we were forced to accept the fact that Jesus was "not in all points tempted as are we," and subject to the limitations of humanity during his earthly ministry.

All this pointed up the conflict which needed resolution at Nicaea. If Jesus were human and divine, was he of the same "substance" as God the Father? The big discussion at Nicaea was on the word in Greek which, with the addition of one letter, can be changed from meaning "substance like to that of God" to "of the same substance as God." Thus, a Greek iota, or letter "i" separated the two contending parties at the council. The word conflict was between *homoiousios* and *homoousios*. The latter word won the day. There are some who may regard the whole thing as splitting hairs and really a waste of time. It, of course, was hardly that. The doctrinal basis for the Christian faith in God through Christ's revelation was here determined.

There is a story which may help us see how important a comma or one letter in a word can really be. The story explains why telegraph and cable companies spell out punctuation marks instead of having just one signal for them as they used to do. At one time there was a code signal for each punctuation mark, according to this story. A wealthy woman was touring Europe. She cabled her husband as follows: "Have found wonderful bracelet. Price seventy-five thousand dollars. May I buy it?" The husband promptly cabled back, "No price too high." She bought the bracelet. Later the husband sued the company and won. Ever since, the users of Morse code have spelled out punctuation. So, the importance of this one letter in the Nicean Creed preparation set the pattern for Christian doctrine for centuries to come.

For, the Nicene Creed asserted that God and Christ were of the same substance. As stated in the *Layman's Guide,* "This was the attempt to say in the philosophy of the time that there is only one God. He is active in creating and sustaining the world (as the Father); he was in Jesus Christ (as the Son); and he moves in the heart of the believer (as the Holy Spirit)." Here is a doctrinal echo expressing what Paul had said in blessing the Corinthians, "The grace of the Lord Jesus Christ, and the love of God, and the fellowship of the Holy Spirit, be with you all."

What the Trinity Says to Us

The expression of Christian belief in the oneness of God expressed in three persons is admittedly a paradox. How can you have one God and three persons within that person? How can any human mind think of three realities in human experience—the reality of God, of man, and of the consciously felt indwelling presence of the Spirit of God? How can we reconcile the idea that God is here and yet "out there," that he is "Holy Other" and yet the divine in the human? How talk of his holiness in one breath and in the next speak of the fellowship of unholy man with Holy God? No wonder we have problems in understanding and in accepting the doctrine of the Trinity!

Dr. Robert South, a seventeenth-century Englishman, was once moved to exclaim, "As he that denies this fundamental article of the Christian religion may lose his soul, so he that strives to understand it may lose his wits." And we know what he means. But Bowie reminds us that "alongside that whimsical expression we must set the words of the German mystic, Gerhard Tersteegen: 'A God understood, a God comprehended, is no God.' That is to say, the greatness and glory of God cannot be caught up in any easy pattern of our thinking. It was not strange then, that those who formulated the doctrine of the Trinity and those who afterwards held it, should have used language that ended in paradox."

We need to try to understand the doctrine of the Trinity because of its central importance in our Christian faith. Theologian William G. T. Shedd, in his introductory essay to *Nicene and Post-Nicene Fathers,* points this up when he writes, "Take out of the Christian consciousness the thoughts and affections that relate to the Father, the Son, and the Holy Spirit, and there is no Christian consciousness left. . . . Mysterious as it is, the Trinity of Divine Revelation is the doctrine that holds in it all the hope of man; for it holds within it the infinite pity of the Incarnation and the infinite mercy of the redemption."

The doctrine of the Trinity can help us see God as person. Many of us are turned off at the outset by trying to conceive of God as person when the Trinitarian doctrine speaks of "Three Persons" but one God. We need to see, first of all, that the word "person" did not mean to the early thinkers what it means today. Three persons today for us would be Tom, Dick, and Harry. According to the *Layman's Guide,* the Latin word *persona* originally referred to a mask which was worn by an actor on the stage to hide his own identity and/or to give identity to the part he was playing. "In Trinitarian thought the 'mask' is not worn by God to hide but to reveal his true character. It is clear when we think of the Trinity we should not try to think of three persons in our sense of the term."

Writing about the controversy that raged around the Council of Nicaea, D. M. Baillie points up the importance of seeing God as personal in *God Was in Christ.* "It is even more important in the modern world to emphasize this truth that God is always and wholly and in every respect *personal.* Nothing in God is impersonal. His Word is personal. His Spirit is personal. Personality in God must indeed be a very different thing from personality in us. But that is because we are far off from being perfectly personal. God is the only perfectly personal Being. So when Christians speak of any one of the *personae* of God, Father, Son or Holy Spirit, they do not say 'It' but 'He' and 'Him.' Yet when they speak of the Triune God, they do not say 'They' and 'Them.' God is three 'Persons,' but He is also the infinite and universal Person in three 'modes of existence.'"

Another helpful contribution of the doctrine of the Trinity is that it helps us see God in three manifestations or forms of self-disclosure. We think of our one God coming to us in three vital, even indispensable ways—God above, God within Christ, incarnate, and God within all men the inspiring, indwelling Presence. We need to take the doctrine seriously because, as Charles Duthie states, "The Trinity enables us to give a more satisfying explanation of God's self-revelation and of our knowledge of Him than any other view."

We can take a page from the experience of the early Christians at this point. We spoke of the fact that the doctrine of the Trinity came out of the experience of the early Christians as a means of explaining the experiences of God which they had found so real. They knew God as the Creator, the Lawgiver, the wise and glorious Moral Governor. But they found God as something far more wonderful; in the words of Dr. Baillie, "Here is the One who *gives* us what He demands of us, *provides* the obedience that He requires; so that we are constrained to acknowledge . . . the paradox of grace." The experience of this paradox came into the lives of these Christians through one whose life was the very life of God himself, and yet at the same time, it was in the fullest sense the life of a man.

Dr. Baillie writes, "Jesus Christ is the One in whom selfhood fully came to its own and lived its fullest life, as human life ought to be lived, because His human selfhood was wholly yielded to God, so that His whole life was the life of God." Then these Christians discovered that what happened in and through Jesus did not end when he was taken from them. Baillie suggests that very soon they made two discoveries. First, that the divine Presence of which they had become aware during the days Jesus was with them "in the flesh" had returned to them, and was to continue with them in a way "that was independent of His actual presence in the flesh, though not independent of His *having* lived on earth in the flesh." Second, they discovered that this experi-

135

ence of the reality of the Holy Spirit, "which depended entirely on Jesus, need not be confined to those who had known Jesus in the flesh. It could come to anybody through the story of Jesus and their witness of its meaning."

Thus, these who had come to know God in Jesus, now came to know him in the Holy Spirit. Go back and read the account of the early days of the Christian Church as they are recorded in the Acts of the Apostles. You cannot read the Book of Acts and fail to recognize there the Holy Spirit as a transfiguring power. The followers of Jesus had found the Holy Spirit as a present and living experience. David Read gives a vivid description in *The Christian Faith:* "This was God alive among them and within them. And by his Spirit everything else came alive—the Scriptures, the Church, themselves."

This has been the experience of Christians across twenty centuries. It is not that they had to accept the doctrine of the Trinity in order to know the God revealed in Jesus. Rather, because they came to know the God of Jesus they found the doctrine of the Trinity a means of expressing what they had found in God the Son and God the Holy Spirit. For we soon learn that this doctrine is intended to affirm, not deny, the oneness of God, as explained by Claude Welch in the *Handbook of Christian Theology.* "It refers to an inner richness or complexity, not dividing God into parts, but describing the nature of his oneness as a living and full unity."

We need always to remember that our understanding of God as Christians is rooted in what we have seen, heard and learned in Jesus Christ. Our insight comes from and through the "Word made flesh." It was what the disciples saw and experienced in their relationship with Jesus which made them aware of God and of what kind of a Heavenly Father he is. Then came the crucifixion. They lived through the agony of darkness as the lights of their world went out when the light of their Life was done to death on the cross. But with Easter Day, here was new experience and re-created life. His living Presence came back to them in risen power—not to just one person or to a group of three or four—but to the whole Christian community. Here they experienced again the greatness and the power as well as the love of God. God touched their lives again through Jesus the risen Lord, as he had through Jesus the Master. And this indwelling Spirit, which diffused through their lives and experience into the lives and experiences of many persons who had never known the man Jesus, brought assurance of God's redeeming love for all men everywhere.

One of those for whom this experience of God in Christ came after Jesus had concluded his earthly ministry was the Apostle Paul. Paul was stopped in his mission to persecute Christians by an arresting vision of Christ on the Damascus Road. He went out then to become a witness to that God who had revealed himself through the Son and who continued to express himself in the indwelling Spirit. So Paul was speaking out of his own experience of the Trinity of God's oneness when he gave the closing blessing assuring the Corinthian Christians of the grace, the love, and the abiding fellowship of God: "The grace of the Lord Jesus Christ, and the love of God, and the fellowship of the Holy Spirit, be with you all."

God Speaks—Prayer

After a recent professional football game, John Wilbur, a rookie guard for the Dallas Cowboys, explained why he had so much trouble containing his opponent, Bill Glass, a Baptist minister who plays guard for Cleveland. Said Wilbur, "He's got speed, size, strength—and besides all that he prays."

When Hurricane Camille accounted for some heavy floods in Virginia in the summer of 1969, the press interviewed a policeman in the area most seriously affected. He reported that an old lady called in to complain that the water was rising rapidly around her house; it was shaking pretty badly, so what should she do? The policeman said he told her "What I have been telling the others—get up high and pray!"

Frank Sinatra is not one of the theological giants of our time. However, he was quoted in *Esquire* as saying what apparently a good many of his fellow countrymen believe, "I'm for anything that gets you through the night, be it prayer, tranquilizers, or a bottle of Jack Daniel."

In *More Than We Are,* Margueritte Harmon Bro tells the story of Cabeza de Vaca, a Spaniard who trekked from Florida to California between 1528 and 1536. At one place, the Indians came to him and his companion asking them to cure the sick. The Indians believed that, being white men, they had superhuman power and could use it if they wanted to. He reported that they were actually two white men who were half starved, lost and despairing, and certainly they felt they had no such healing power. "But, we had to heal them or die," he wrote. "So we prayed for strength. We prayed on bended knees and in an agony of hunger." Then they blessed each ailing Indian—and saw that the sick were indeed being healed. "Truly it was to our amazement that the ailing said they were well. Being Europeans, we thought we had given away to doctors and priests our ability to heal. But here it was, still in our possession . . . It was ours after all; we were more than we thought we were . . . To be more than I thought I was—a sensation utterly new to me."

Prayer and praying are the common elements in these four instances, but how discouraging to try to understand prayer as a Christian and reconcile it with the startling differences reflected in these accounts.

139

Much That Passes for Prayer—

Many persons simply give up on the idea of prayer. And it is hard to blame them because of some of the things that are passed off as being a legitimate part of the prayer process. Much of this is irrational, superstitious and self-centered, and therefore unworthy of the pattern of prayer one finds in Jesus. The problem comes when one gets hold of a half truth and lifts it to the level of ultimate truth. As we observed elsewhere, it is partially true, but substantially incorrect.

Take the persons who build on the idea of a personal God and reduce God to a benevolent grandfather. In the cartoon strip "Wee Pals," two youngsters are hoping it doesn't rain on their picnic next month. One lad inquires, "Why don't you phone the weatherman to order some sunshine for that day." The haughty reply of the older child is, "Only the man upstairs can do that, Wellington!" And the boy's final question is simple, "What's his phone number?"

You are thinking, "They are just children now. They will learn." Will they? Football games in some sections of our country are preceded by an invocation which often includes language appropriate to the situation, like "that great Quarterback in the sky." I am glad I have never been faced with the chore of preparing such an invocation. It has some real dilemmas. At one televised, Big Eight game last year, the clergyman concluded his prayer: "And dear Lord, we invite You to take time out from Your busy schedule to watch our game this afternoon." Seconds later a telephone rang in the press box, and a fellow sitting there commented, "God wants to know what channel it is on." Is the latter more outlandish than the former?

Then there are persons who in apparent sincerity really do clothe the silly with sanctity and the ridiculous with a pseudopiety. Charley Brown, that widely known theologian of the comic strip, once reported to Lucy as he knelt beside his bed for prayer, "I think I've made a new theological discovery. If you hold your hands upside down, you get the opposite of what you pray for." Before you dismiss that as a childish immaturity, listen to what a group called the "Religious Research Foundation of America" did at the World Council of Churches session in Evanston. A. Leonard Griffith tells the story in *What Is a Christian*. Unofficially, the foundation (not related at all to the WCC) set up a display in a hotel lobby nearby. It consisted of two pie plates, one filled with barren dirt and the other with a tiny garden. Seeds had been planted in both plates and both had been carefully watered. But it seems that a group of people had prayed that one set of seeds would germinate and grow, and the other set would die. The prayer experiment having proved "successful," they now wanted the church to pay attention. More a primitive form of voodooism than prayer, wouldn't you say? An insult to Almighty God are such petitions unrelated to human need, and which call for this kind of "religious hocus pocus."

Few of us have not at times used prayer as a means of using God. We want him to bless our efforts, whatever they are and however far they may be from God-like living. D. T. Niles tells of a friend of his, a pastor in Ceylon, who reported

141

something that happened to persons in his congregation. A man had made love to his friend's wife and both the man and woman had run away from their mates to live together outside marriage. This man told his pastor that on their first night together both he and the woman had knelt together and prayed. And he said, "We never felt nearer to God."

All of which suggests that understanding prayer as a Christian is not a simple task. To say the word "prayer," to encourage all persons to "pray" can mean so many different things to so many different people. How can we sift through all the straw of misuse of prayer to find the grains of what Jesus talked about, what he lived, and what he called us to practice?

Jerome Beatty tells a ludicrous story of the fellow in New York who answered his telephone one day and heard the following: "This is a recording. You have answered an incorrect phone call. Please hang up and make sure the next time to answer a correct call. Thank you." That gets more absurd the more you think about it. Yet, there are some strange parallels there to the way in which man responds to God's call in and through prayer.

Ways of Getting Our Wishes

"There are three ways a man gets what he wants in life: thinking, working, and praying," says Harry Emerson Fosdick in *Living Under Tension*. Do you agree? The use of mind, of muscle, and of spiritual dynamic are all essential to effective survival for humankind. And only praying is ritualized among these three. This results in the abandonment of prayer by many persons for whom it seems but a formal, conventional, technically religious performance that they do not understand. Thus, they are left with only two ways of fulfilling their life's desires—thinking and working. They think and they work and hope that will be enough. Sometimes it falls far short of being enough. For there are none of those deep interior resources of inspiration and spiritual intake without which few powerful personalities are ever achieved.

Among these thinking persons, there are some who argue that prayer is theoretically irrational. One cannot reason himself into an intellectual acceptance of the rationality of prayer, they say. Yet, in the next breath such persons may admit, as many such have admitted to me, that there are times when they honestly wish they could know how to pray.

There are persons, at least one of whom is known by every man, who no longer argue about prayer. They have found in prayer a sustaining source of power which nonprayers never seem to have. Dr. Fosdick speaks of them, "Call it what we will, we find in every great soul something that goes beyond thinking and working—inner receptivity, sensitiveness and hospitality to a world of truth and power higher than the self."

So, you think prayer is nonsense—irrational in your world of philosophical reality? But while you protest, I keep remembering those who have found reality in prayer, my parents, teachers, parishioners being among these. Or, take some man of the world like Henry M. Stanley, a hard-living newsman who found David Livingstone in Africa. Coming out of the perils he found in the heart of the dark continent, Stanley reported that "prayer made him stronger morally and mentally than all his non-praying companions and lifted him hopefully over the wilderness of forest tracks, eager for each day's labors and fatigues."

What I am asking here is simply this: Is there a reader who, observing some person strengthened by the power of prayer, doesn't join me in asking, "What is that force? Don't worry about naming it. Just tell us what this power is, and how one gets into contact with it and handles it? How *does* one learn to pray?"

This was the question of the disciples as they sought of Jesus an answer. They said simply, "Lord, teach us to pray." Jesus in his life and teaching set forth some essential elements in the process. As we look at them, we find we must feel a deep sense of need first of all. We need to know just what prayer really is. We find the pattern for prayer in Jesus of whom we make our request, "Teach us to pray."

Deep Sense of Need

There are basically two ways to learn to pray. The first is to "argue it out." In this intellectual process we deal with all our doubts and try to dissolve them. We reason out a solution to each of the problems concerning prayer. We try to get all our questions answered. Then we pray or not, depending on our final reasoning concerning prayer. I presume many folks have arrived at a satisfactory practice of prayer by this process. But too many others are still in the rationalizing process. And life is hastening by with no interior resources developed for the long pull of life's problems.

Perhaps we are too demanding of ourselves if we use this way of learning to pray. If we have to wait until we know all the involved process by which electricity is provided for lighting a dark room before we turn the switch, we will probably, most of us anyway, remain in the dark. If you require of yourself that you understand all the intricacies of the process by which sound and picture are transmitted from a studio to your living room before you turn on your set, you will never listen to radio and never watch television. While that may be a blessing, the illustration is to the point that we don't have to be able to explain fully the nature of God in order to make contact with him through prayer.

Actually, the second way to learn to pray is the more effective. Stated simply, it is to reach that point where we sense a need of backing and support in life greater than our own strength, so we reach out to God and find him there. This was the point that day when the disciples asked simply, "Lord teach us to pray." Yes, the first essential in learning to pray is to feel deeply our own need for prayer. If we struggle with it only on an intellectual level and need all our rational t's crossed and logical i's dotted before we start praying, we may be defeated at the outset. If there is not a felt need, there will be no adequate motive for using the prayer resources.

To be sure, there are some who feel no such need. They are getting by in life pretty well with thinking and working. But one day each of us comes to the point where he longs for the assurance, the survival power, the dynamic for daily life which praying persons seem to have. And when that day comes we can take the first step in the process of learning to pray. Few of us I suppose, in our professional or vocational jobs, feel the need for higher mathematics. We can go on for months and seldom if ever think about higher math. But if we are engineers we soon face up to our need for it. If we are charged with building a span like the Big Mac bridge across the Straits of Mackinac, then we soon face the fact that you don't get very far in bridge building without the knowledge of the resources of higher math. The point is equally true in building the structure of an effective life for our time. You don't get very far before you run into the demand for resources of higher spiritual power.

Sometimes it takes something dramatic to bring us to our sense of need. Nobel peace prize winner, Albert Luthuli, the African leader, tells in his autobiography, *Let My People Go,* of his imprisonment for his dissent from the discriminatory political structure of his nation. He was in solitary confinement and not even the warders who brought his meals could speak to him. Illness kept him confined to his lonely bed. He wrote, "Nevertheless, I do not remember my cell as a place of boredom. It became, in fact, a place of sanctuary, a place where I could make up for the neglect of religious meditation occasioned by the hurly-burly of public life. There was time, there was quietness, there was comparative solitude. I used it. Frail man that I am, I pray humbly that I may never forget the opportunity God gave me to rededicate myself, to consider the problems of our resistance to bondage, and above all to be quiet in His Presence. My whitewashed cell became my chapel, my place of retreat." Few of us, I suppose, would find this kind of spiritual resource unless we, too, were forced into a kind of solitary confinement away from our busy world.

If the conscious need for the power that prayer can bring into life does not arise for you in the daily pattern of your living, it is unlikely that you will continue long to escape two particular experiences. They call out a conscious need for the deeper kind of prayer which provides those interior resources that alone enable one to stand in the time of testing.

Take the matter of being up against more than we can master alone. Two athletic teams may be on equal terms for three quarters of a game. They are equally good. But, one team is good a little longer than the other and emerges victorious. Many of the trying experiences of life can be taken in stride by all of us because we have the stoic strength to shrug them off. But one day we come to a test of our endurance for which we find no resources available. Tragedy strikes as it did in our community recently with the death of a school boy on the hockey rink. It leaves a whole school of youngsters and teachers stunned by its stark suddenness. And the tragedy causes many of us, who do not personally know the individuals involved, that kind of heartsickness that is the mark of human identification with those who have suffered loss and sorrow. Do you believe that thinking and working alone will produce the kind of interior resources one needs for endurance against this kind of experience?

Or what of the times you have pronounced your efforts, perchance your life, a failure? What brought you back from despair or the thought of self-destruction? Was it that you

147

used reason and logic to dispel your depression? I hope you did, for they can be helpful. But the folks I know who have ultimately overcome such experiences are those who tapped the deep interior resources of spiritual vitality which are reached only through faith and prayer.

A second experience that few of us can escape in the ordinary run of life is that of undertaking tasks which prove too difficult for us to accomplish alone and solely on our human dimension of strength. I recall as a boy helping my father try to lower a heavy box from the garage attic. After we had pushed it free of the attic shelf out into the open space above the garage floor, we found that our combined strength was not enough to hold the awkward box. We tried, but it slipped and crashed on the concrete floor. But, not before it accounted for a sprained wrist on my part and badly skinned shins for my father. We simply took on too much for our own human lifting power. Don't you and I do that every day when it comes to the demanding experiences of life in our time? The difference in the situations is that there are interior resources available for every one of us in dealing with the loads of life. We can tap those resources through prayer when we have that kind of deep sense of need which leads us eagerly to seek to hear God speak to us in prayer.

Know What Prayer Is!

We need to face the fact that for some persons prayer is but a "pious sigh, warranted in petitions for better weather, tax relief, a lower golf score, or an end to suffering," as someone has put it. And that kind of prayer releases very little of the power which the spiritual resources within human personality can provide.

We do not know what prayer is until we realize that prayer is not petition centered solely on our own wish or need. Prayer is not selfish begging. Yet, for many of us, this is about the only level of prayer we have consciously experienced. And finding nothing of what Jesus talked about as being a part of prayer, we abandon it as useless in our life situation.

For example, we talk about praying for peace and justice, but too often we introduce our own personal ideas about what peace should be and justice is—in other words, it is what we want it to be and that's what we pray for. If as Elizabeth Barrett Browning put it, "every wish is like a prayer, with God," then Dr. Fosdick is correct when he says that millions of Americans are not praying for peace or justice. Many of our people are praying,

> Bless me and my wife
> Our son John and his wife,
> Us four, no more. Amen.

Erma Bombeck, a housewife from Dayton, Ohio, is a popular newspaper columnist. She has a knack for finding the funny bone in many of the normal experiences of daily life. Recently she entitled her column, "Some Simple Prayers Help Mom Survive the Summer." Then she, in prayer parodies, offers petitions concerning mosquitoes, a visit to the dentist, the appearance of her youngster in church, the driving inability of her husband. Anyone of us could have offered the final prayer, "Please God, have I ever called upon you for a biggie? When my washer overflowed, didn't I offer to build an ark? When I burnt the first communion chicken didn't I laugh? (Ho, Ho, remember?) All I am asking, before I go into the room filled with the Class of 1949, is to make me look thin. You can do it. (You are the only one who can do it.) Do you know what it is to suck in your stomach and have nothing move? Please Lord, dim the lights, crush me in the crowd. And if you can't make me thin, Lord, on such short notice, could you please make Eloise Heartfly look fat?"

These speak to us "where we live," because most of us are guilty of praying such prayers, of thinking such thoughts, and of doing so without the tongue-in-cheek approach of both these writers. Certainly the Christian sees that prayer must be more than this. It has to move above the level of selfish begging to be even a simple prayer of petition. It must go beyond the circle of self-concern and avoid concentration on the fulfillment of our own selfish wishes. Only then does it approach the edge of the spiritual dynamic which the saints seem to have found through prayer.

In answering his disciples' request, Jesus took more time than merely the recorded answer of the moment. He spent his ministry teaching his disciples about prayer. He taught them that prayer is the means whereby we enter into communion with our Heavenly Father to make it possible for God to do for us, and to us, and in us what he wills to have done. But this depends on our own receptivity. It requires our own willingness to see that prayer is not something we are called to do for God so God will treat us right. Rather, prayer is the means whereby we open our lives for God's will to be done in and through us. Meister Eckhart, a German monk of the fourteenth century, explained the nature of prayer in arresting simplicity when he wrote, "God is bound to act, to pour himself into thee as soon as He find thee ready."

Prayer for Jesus is the means for realization of the God-power within you. Because Harry Emerson Fosdick, through his preaching and his books, particularly his classic, *The Meaning of Prayer,* has been most helpful to me, as to many persons, in understanding how God meets our needs through prayer, you find repeated reference to him in these pages. For example, note what he wrote about realizing the God-power in us: "Prayer is inwardly fulfilling conditions so that power is released. I do not believe in miracles in the old terms of broken or suspended law, but I have to believe in (these) scientific miracles, incredible things done by science through the releasing of cosmic power; and I have to believe in personal miracles, incredible things happening in people and to people and for people who have liberated the divine resources." Prayer is the means not only of discovering these interior resources which Jesus knew, but it is also the means of releasing them into the bloodstream of life that we might know their power as Jesus knew it from the prayers of his life.

Prayer is communion with our Heavenly Father, said Jesus. It is the endeavor to put ourselves in such a relationship with God that he can do in us and for us and through us what he wants to do. One shares this communion in the warmth and intimacy of personal relationship through prayer. It is not a time when we seek to bend God's will to ours. Through prayer we seek to learn God's will for us and to find at the same time the strength and fortitude to do that will.

The Pattern for Prayer in Jesus

In Jesus' answer to the disciples' question, they found not only the words of what we know as the Lord's Prayer, but they came to see in their Master the living pattern of what prayer is. Once again, read Dr. Fosdick's comment on this scene with its question and answer in *The Secret of Victorious Living:* "Note that this awakened interest in prayer came not at all from new arguments about it but from a new exhibition of its power. Here before their very eyes they saw a personality in whom prayer was vital and influential. The more they lived with him the more they saw that they never could explain him unless they understood his praying, and so, not at all because of new arguments, but because of amazing spiritual power released in him by prayer, they wanted him to tell them how to pray." The disciples saw how Jesus prayed, as we can see, and they learned as can we, what the elements are that lead to an effectual prayer life.

Jesus prayed *regularly.* The disciples had observed those hours of prayer when Jesus turned aside from the crowd to be alone in meditation. Indeed, they all belonged to a religious family which emphasized regularity in prayers. As a Hebrew, one prayed at regular intervals throughout the day—early morning, noon, afternoon, evening, and nighttime. There are prescribed prayers and practices that the faithful Jew follows. Jesus came into this pattern of prayer honestly as an inheritance. He found that regular times of prayer, faithfully observed, could produce the kind of vitality in one's spiritual life, the kind of dynamic in one's religious living, the kind of depth in one's awareness of God that is not possible in the hit-and-miss procedure which most of us use in our pattern of prayer. One does not stand the stresses of life when they come, simply by resorting to prayer in moments of extremity. One builds strength for stress as did Jesus, through the daily pattern of private prayer and the regular participation in corporate worship and prayer in the church.

Jesus prayed *receptively*. The Scripture record offers much insight into the prayer life of our Lord Jesus. He did not demand the same spot for each time of prayer. He found some places particularly meaningful for his prayer time. Thus he went to the mountaintop, to the desert, to the garden, to the temple, to the lakeshore—the place was not the important item so much as the process by which he found prayer-strength. He prayed receptively with "hospitality of the soul in entertaining the most high." If prayer were that for us, think what a dimension could be added to our lives. If we really believed that when we pray we are indeed extending the hospitality of our soul to the highest of all, then prayer could well bring us spiritual strength like that which we have never before experienced in prayer.

Will power is not enough to get the job done, Jesus would say. We need a sensitized openness to God's spirit before we can know the conscious awareness that our lives are vitally linked with God.

This can come about only as we consciously seek to make our lives more God-centered and less self-centered. Thus, we pray receptively as Jesus did. We wait to hear God's word for us. We sublimate our own desires and wishes for blessings of the moment to the realization that the real power of prayer is in communion and interaction with our Heavenly Father through the conversation of prayer.

Jesus prayed *affirmatively*. This is something more than positive thinking. It is something more than empty optimism. To pray affirmatively calls for something more than selfishly begging God to grant our wishes. It is to affirm our faith in God and our willingness to take from him both the blessings of life and the demands of his divine will for our life. Real prayer is affirmation. Many Scripture writers knew this and expressed it.

> Even though I walk through the valley of
>   the shadow of death,
> I fear no evil;
> for thou art with me.
>
> (Ps. 23:4)

> God is our refuge and strength,
>   a very present help in trouble.
> Therefore we will not fear though the earth
>   should change,
>   though the mountains shake in the heart
>   of the sea;

The Lord of hosts is with us;
   the God of Jacob is our refuge.
                      (Ps. 46:1-2, 7)

They who wait for the Lord shall renew
    their strength,
   they shall mount up with wings as eagles,
they shall run and not be weary,
   they shall walk, and not faint.
                      (Isa. 40:31)

Likewise the Spirit helps us in our weakness; for we do not know how to pray as we ought, but the Spirit himself intercedes for us with sighs too deep for words. . . . We know that in everything God works for good with those who love him, who are called according to his purpose.

                      (Rom. 8:26, 28)

Do you see what it is to pray with affirmation? It brings into the very center of our souls the convictions and reassurances that crowd out our fears and our anxieties. Jesus could never have lived without this.

This is, moreover, praying with an intelligent common sense. Jesus did not pray for that which was patently impossible. He asked for the cup of the cross to pass. He prayerfully explored ways of doing God's will without the cross. But, always he came back to face it and accept it. How easy to pray that God will send peace into our world, and yet at the same time escalate our efforts to wage war. How easy it is to blurt out a desperate prayer, "O Lord make the brakes hold," when we are going eighty miles an hour and suddenly face a need for a quick stop to avoid hitting another car. Not much intelligence in such a prayer, not much common sense. Not much of the kind of affirmative prayer which Jesus prayed.

Better one should pray with the insight of poet Robert Freeman:

> White Captain of my soul, lead on;
> I follow Thee, come dark or dawn
> Only vouchsafe three things I crave:
> Where terror stalks, help me be brave!
> Where righteous ones can scarce endure
> The siren call, help me be pure!
> Where vows grow dim, and men dare do
> What once they scorned, help me be true.[1]

Finally, note that Jesus prayed *faithfully*. Not only was his life one of unceasing prayerfulness, but he prayed with fidelity. When God spoke to him and called him to mission, Jesus was ready and enabled of God to do what was called for. He was willing to pray dangerously—the danger that one will find an inner compulsion from the divine will which will send him to Calvary and a cross. Are you willing to risk the peril of a dangerous prayer? God may call you to accept the obligation to move out into an area of Christian witness which risks, if not your life, perchance your popularity, or your acceptance by certain peers, or your security. To learn to

---

[1] "Prayer" in *I Quote*, ed. Virginia Ely (New York: George Stewart, 1947), p. 29.

pray is not to make life easy. It may well make life more difficult than before. But it is to know that God matched every challenge to Jesus with strength to meet that challenge. For every divine demand, there was a new dimension of divine strength added to Jesus' own strength. And so it can be for us today, said Jesus, if we maintain fidelity in fulfilling God's will for us.

My guide in the Garden of Gethsemane assured me that one of the olive trees there is more than two thousand years old. The others are later additions since the time of Christ. I stood beside that oldest tree and tried to see Jesus there, tried to realize that presumably he could have stood where I was standing. What prayer was it he breathed or spoke beneath this particular tree? Whatever it was, I know one thing: it included the inevitable word for the Christian prayer—"Not my will but thine be done." I lifted my gaze. I could see above the walls of Jerusalem the place called Mount Calvary. And I knew then, as I know now, that it was the prayer of Jesus, here in Gethsemane, that girded him finally for the demands there on the cross. Richard C. Trench's prayer-poem expresses this strength which comes through prayer:

> Lord, what a change within us one short hour
> Spent in Thy presence will prevail to make!
> What heavy burdens from our bosoms take,
> What parched grounds refresh as with a shower!
> We kneel, and all around us seems to lower;
> We rise, and all, the distant and the near,
> Stands forth in sunny outline brave and clear;
> We kneel, how weak! we rise, how full of power!

God Re-creates—Resurrection

"Jesus said, 'I am the resurrection and the life, whoever believes in me will live, even though he dies; and whoever lives and believes in me will never die."

These were the first words heard at the funeral services of General Eisenhower in Washington Cathedral. Jesus said, "I am the resurrection and the life." Believe this and live life that will never end. Live this faith and death can have no ultimate power over you.

Now, whether or not you heard these words with anything more than a casual interest in them as part of the pageantry of a state funeral, you must realize that they force you to face a proposition that makes you choose one way or the other. You cannot avoid the encounter. You must opt one way or the other on the proposition as stated by Professor Montague: "Are the things we care for most at the mercy of the things we care for least?" The answer you give that question makes world's of difference for your world.

When the Spaniards first set foot in America, they were elated after their dangerous voyage across uncharted seas. Archer Wallace reports they sent back word to Spain they had reached the outer limit of the world. They could conceive of nothing beyond where they were. Spain rejoiced that their explorers had reached the ends of the earth. Coins were minted to commemorate this achievement. The words on them said "Ne Plus Ultra," meaning "no more beyond."

Pity the poor coiners when, within a month after these coins were put into circulation, daring men had crossed this continent and were standing on the western shores looking out on the surging Pacific. There was more beyond! So, hastily, coins were called back and reminted with the words, "Plus Ultra"—"more beyond."

Now, there are many folks today who feel that man has about reached the end of his explorations in life. As they sing in the musical *Oklahoma* about the city where my parents lived for many years, "In Kansas City, they've gone about as far as they can go." Many persons say that about life here and now. This is it. We have gone as far as there is to go. "Nothing beyond!"

Easter comes each year to remind us that the Christian faith believes there is indeed more beyond this world, that man has not exhausted his possibilities for growth, that death and the grave are not the end of life. Easter celebrates the victory over death of one who said, "I am the resurrection and the life, he who believes in me, though he dies, yet shall he live" (John 11:25). Here is a glorious fact to be believed, a crucial issue to be faced, and a decisive event under which we are called to live.

Glorious Fact

The Resurrection is a glorious fact to be believed. You cannot account for the Christian church without it. To be sure, we really talk very little about the Resurrection. I suspect this is because we don't want to talk much about death. But we need to see that this does not necessarily involve a physical resurrection. I find no scriptural grounds for such a demand. In fact, the Apostle Paul says just the opposite. He had no doubts about the Resurrection of Jesus. He had not seen him in life, but he believed what the disciples had reported concerning his post mortem appearances to them—very much alive. But, Paul never suggests, nor even implies, that Jesus after death appeared in a body of flesh and blood. In I Corinthians, Paul discusses the difference between the "physical body" and the "spiritual body." Ernest F. Tittle commented on this in *A Mighty Fortress,* "What Paul envisages in the life to come is not the resurrection of the body laid in the grave, but is the acquisition from God of a new kind of body adapted to the conditions of a world transcending the physical demands and limitations of an earthly existence."

Quickly we need to see that faith in the Resurrection is faith alone. One would be hard put to prove the Resurrection as a

160

fact from a scientific standpoint. In fact, he is destined for frustration who seeks to base his faith on such proof. Yet, before you dismiss this as negative proof, recall how many things which are real to you that cannot be proved among the test-tube and bunsen-burner set! What about the reality of love—ever captured it in a test tube, or net, or little box? How about loyalty—what kind of vivisection did you make of it as you ran down its roots of reality? Patriotism—is that something for scientific proof in some laboratory? Yet love and loyalty and patriotism are very real feelings which come as the result of our affection for another person, or our gratitude for our nation, or our response to the call of the highest within us for ultimate loyalty. How do we prove the validity of these very real feelings and experiences known to most of us as scientifically tested facts? Yet, do you deny their reality in your life or question them in mine?

This, of course, is not to say that we are without evidence in support of the Christian concept of Resurrection. Our evidence is in three parts. First, there is the fact of the empty tomb. Guards, Romans, and countrymen, as well as the disciples and the women who followed Jesus, all attested to the fact that there was no dead body in the tomb where hours before they had placed the body of Jesus. The gaping hole at the entrance told of an exit, there being no other opening. But some would say, "Anyone could have broken the seal and robbed the grave of its lifeless corpse without having to accept this idea of being raised from the dead." And you are correct. But looked at in simple logic, does it not follow that if there were evidence to support the idea the body was stolen, that the Jewish hierarchy, not to mention Rome and Pilate, would not have hesitated to use that knowledge in its effort to stamp out the Christian faith. Do you find any record they did so?

So, consider with me the second evidence which supports the first. The Resurrection became the central emphasis in apostolic preaching. Travel with the Apostle Paul, with Simon Peter, with Barnabas, with Dr. Luke, and listen in to what they are saying. If you made a tape of any message, you would find in and out of every paragraph the central thread of the Resurrection theme. "He is not here, he is risen." That's what the apostles preached. H. Richard Niebuhr once put it, "We can no longer think of Jesus' purported rising from the dead as a simple instance of miracle, because the whole gospel appears to be rooted in that very tradition." Everywhere the disciples went, the sound was sure to go— "Him whom you killed, God has restored to life again." The conquered had become the conqueror. And this through the Resurrection alone. Remember, the early Christians were martyred by Rome, not because they dared to talk about love and peace and goodwill, but because they dared to state clearly and for all to hear that they hinged their faith on the fact of Jesus' resurrection.

This leads us then very quickly to observe the transformation which took place in these sacred-to-death disciples who became declare-to-the-death apostles of a Resurrection faith. After the crucifixion these men had scattered quickly. Their most courageous member apparently at that time was Simon Peter. "He followed afar off." Yet, staying nearby during the grisly proceedings in Pilate's castle, Peter denied he even knew the Man Jesus when they put him on the spot around the courtyard fire. He saw too clearly for comfort how much of his protestations of loyalty to Jesus on previous occasions were patently bluff. But this same man who makes such a cowardly denial in a crucial moment of testing and runs away from his shame as well as his danger—where is he seven weeks hence? He is standing in the midst of people from all over the empire and clearly and pointedly speaking concerning the central fact of his Christian faith, the Resurrection of Jesus. His sermon at Pentecost closes, "This Jesus God God raised up, and of that we all are witnesses. . . . he has poured out this which you see and hear." (Read Acts 2:14-39.)

Peter was not the only one. In the words of Walter Russell Bowie, "These men, so helpless, so empty-hearted, so broken on the day of the crucifixion, became transformed, every one of them. They moved with confidence in a re-created world. They knew that Jesus was stronger than those who attempted to silence him. He was alive. He would live in them, and they would go forth adventurously to conquer new worlds."

Yes, these were those who were to face death again and again with the confidence and composure of a great faith. Eugene O'Neill captured something of this spirit of courageous disregard for what death can do in his play about Lazarus, the brother of Martha and Mary who, the biblical record reports, was raised from the dead by Jesus. Lazarus leaves home in Bethany and goes to Greece. In Athens he meets the half-crazed and cruel Gaius Caligula whom Tiberius Caesar had chosen as his successor. Caligula is the man who, when informed that people hated him, replied, "Let them hate—so long as they fear us. We must keep death dangling before their eyes—I like to watch men die." When Caligula is confronted by Lazarus, he says, "So, you're the man who teaches people to laugh at death—I fear everyone who lives." But Lazarus looks into the face of the crazed and cruel ruler and laughs softly "like a man in love with God." He says, "Death is dead, Caligula, death is dead." The Caesar-to-be cries out, "You have murdered my only friend, Lazarus; Death would have been my friend when I am Caesar."

Make what you will of that, Lazarus speaks in the authentic Christian faith. The resurrection of Jesus made the early Christians fearless in the face of death. Thus, they were completely unconquerable by the Caligulas of that time.

Crucial Issue

Easter focuses on a crucial issue to be faced by every person. It is not merely peripheral for today's citizen. It is not a far-off impossible dream which belongs to the ancient past with no relevancy for our day. You cannot avoid encounter with the Easter faith. To be sure, you can choose to take it or leave it. But face it, you must. And you cannot dismiss it by pointing to fruitless arguments among professed Christians over the mode of the resurrection of Jesus—natural, spiritual, or no real resurrection at all. A recent editorial in *The Christian Century* points up that these "are essentially an elaborate evasion of the one truly relevant theological question: Since Christ lives, since we have been set free from the perils of the world's hostility by God's assurance that our lives are eternally secure, and since we have been commanded to love, how is it that the church is not alive unto the cross?" How is it that we are not among the disciples who were transformed by the fact of the Resurrection? What kind of witness do we give to the fact that God has redeemed us through a risen Christ? We must face the crucial issue one way or another.

The relevance of the Resurrection can quickly be seen when you point out that without it there would be no Bible, no church, and no Christian faith. Paul stated it with sharp clarity: "And if Christ was not raised, your faith is a delusion; you are still under the control of your sins." (Read I Cor. 15:16-23 Goodspeed.) Consider what history might have been without the Bible, the church, and the Christian faith, all dependent on this key doctrine of the Resurrection, and realize the relevance of this for us—whatever we may be willing to accept or not to accept of the doctrine itself.

It should be of interest if for no other reason than that the fact of death is so much a part of our lives. Thousands of lives have been lost in the fruitless war in Viet Nam. Every day we read of new victims of highway murder-by-auto. This year the number of deaths on highways will approximate more than half the population of the city in which I live. Think of the thousands of deaths from disease. This week in our parish an old man died of cancer and a fifteen-year-old lad died of leukemia, barely three months after it was diagnosed. The television screen brings us the stark pictures of human hunger and starvation. Yes, we cannot escape the fact of death whatever we may do to try to escape it or disguise it. Any person who has reached the age of eighty today has been a part of the world during a time when between two and three billion persons have died. Death is clearly something we have to meet, whether we like it or not.

And our reaction to death, our attitude toward it, becomes determinative for much of our life. However philosophical or fatalistic we may wax in our statements about death, the fact is that here is one of life's crucial issues. A seminary classmate of mine, Tex Evans, has often been likened to Will Rogers because of his droll, whimsical humor. He tells a story on himself which relates that one of his youngsters asked his wife, "Mamma, if Daddy should die, do you reckon there's another man in the world just like him?" And his mother answered, "Maybe there is, son. And it would be just my luck to get him."

We smile, not because we are courageous in the face of a discussion of death, but because death and its discussion makes us nervous. Your attitude here is crucial because it will determine what kind of a life you will live, what meaning or significance you will find in it. The earliest historian in the British Isles is known only as The Venerable Bede. He wrote about a man who described life as "the flight of a sparrow out of darkness across a lighted banquet hall into darkness." Is that the way life appears to you? Not if you are Christian in your perspective on life and death. According to Ernest F. Tittle, "If Christ was indeed raised from the dead, then life is not meaningless and futile, but has set before it an end, a goal, a triumph in which the human spirit can rejoice."

This is a crucial issue because our response to it determines what kind of life we will have and what kind of a world. What you believe about the Resurrection determines the kind of God you worship and also the kind of belief you have about yourself as a person. John Short comments in *The Interpreter's Bible,* "Christian doctrine is not one of immortality, but of resurrection. As expounded by the Apostle Paul, man's hope of survival depends not on the inherent immortality of his soul, but on the act of God. . . . Immortality is the gift of God's grace in response to man's faith."

Henry Sloane Coffin was one of our nation's great preachers. To know him was to know a man transformed by his faith in God's power given man in Christ. Speaking of the Resurrection as a means of our understanding the nature of the God revealed through Jesus Christ, Dr. Coffin wrote, "Easter is the festival of the trustworthiness of God for those who confide in him." Understanding what the Resurrection is and what it means, we can understand something of what God is and what God does. "Resurrection means return in power, despite death and burial, and going on with divine force in and through His Church, His Body."

What you believe about the Resurrection determines what you believe about man as well as God. Either you believe man is of infinite spiritual worth because his life is the gift of God, or you believe man is but a machine with only a mechanistic or materialistic explanation for his existence. Dr. Fosdick reported a conversation which he had during World War II. He talked with an American journalist who had covered the news in Berlin up to the moment of America's entrance into the war. The newsman told the New York preacher, "I came home from Berlin and went back to my old college campus, and I said to some of the professors there, 'You are teaching these students here the philosophy that has made Nazi Germany what she is. You tried to teach me that only a few years ago—a godless materialism that makes the physical the source and end of everything, that undermines the bases of moral principle and makes of the whole universe a purposeless machine. And now in Nazidom I have seen what happens when that philosophy really gets going and comes to its logical conclusion. And I have come back to tell you that the stuff you are teaching here is about the most dangerous dynamite that is being scattered around the world.'"

Our free republic rests on the deep conviction that the human life is inherently of infinite dignity and value and possibility. A materialistic philosophy which denies the existence of God and the possibility of resurrection will change the whole climate of a man's thought and way of life.

There are fakirs in India who can throw colored dust on a pool of water in such a way as to form the portrait of distinguished persons. The picture remains until a breeze ruffles the water. Then the face disappears. Is this what God does? Does he create a Plato or a Socrates, or an Isaiah or a Jesus, or one of your loved ones now gone—and then let the gentle breeze of dying or sharp wind of death blot them out forever? The Christian answer comes, "By his great mercy we have been born anew to a living hope through the resurrection of Jesus Christ from the dead." (I Pet. 1:3.)

Decisive Event

Easter brings us repeatedly to face a decisive event under which every Christian is called to live. There are some who quietly ignore the event. They live as if it hadn't happened. They refuse to face it in any perspective. They just assume it didn't happen and that's an end to that.

Others may come to grips with it but they disbelieve it. Now there is no reason to be smug about our willingness to believe and to look down on those who disbelieve as some kind of second-class citizens. The future is not easy to believe in. Every step of man's progress has had its majority share of unbelievers in the generations which preceded that event or act which marked progress. It can be illustrated with a bishop of one of the denominations out of which has come The United Methodist Church. At the turn of the twentieth century he was visiting a denominational college in the west. The president, who doubled as a physics teacher, invited some members of the faculty in to share an informal hour with the bishop. The president asked the bishop his opinion as to the next major advances he thought man would make. The bishop pontificated that every thing worth inventing had already been produced and that man's progress was at an end (a not uncommon conviction in those days). The young president quietly objected and felt there were many exciting advances which man would yet make. "Name one," the bishop challenged. "Well," he replied, "for one thing I think that in our lifetime man will fly in the air like birds." Now get the bishop's answer. "Nonsense, if God ever intended man to fly in the air, he would have given him wings in the first place." There's a trailer to the story which gives it even more punch. The bishop was from Dayton, Ohio. His name was Wright. In fact, he was the father of Orville and Wilbur Wright, who first fulfilled the young college president's prediction.

Some face the issue and refuse to decide for or against it. They do not disbelieve the fact of the Resurrection, but they cannot actually accept it. There is an enviable honesty in an agnosticism which says, "I cannot yet tell. I won't deny it, but by the same token I won't believe it." One could argue this all day and get nowhere. I guess I will just say that I am glad the apostles were not agnostics. Had they been, they would still be hovering over a decision and the world would have gone off and left them. And what a sorry world we would then have been bequeathed.

Some—probably more than you might suspect—believe the Resurrection. One cannot stay long at a halfway house of indecision. He must vote it up or down sooner or later. If we can find a faith in God strong enough, then we need have no further fear of anything that could happen to us, even death. Roland Hayes' mother, Angel Mo', was born into slavery. Her constant encouragement and sacrifice made possible the marvelous contributions represented in his life and Christian witness. Shortly before she died, she wrote her son, "You must not feel sad when the Lord comes to take me away—if I am who I say I am, I will be better off." Well, are we who we say we are?

We need to grant that one of the reasons some are re-

reluctant about Resurrection is the fact they think of it as a mere continuation of life here into the life hereafter. Like the Egyptian mummies, they wonder if it isn't a good idea to take with you to your grave your earthly possessions for use over on the other side. A man had a Brink's truck in his funeral procession carrying his money to the grave with the body. This prompted the comment from a bystander, "He said he would show them he could take it with him." But we know that it is carrying it to an extreme to imagine this kind of other world. Yet the idea of continuation of sameness will not down. We can understand the fellow Maude Royden told about, who wanted his epitaph to read:

> Don't bother me now
> Don't bother me ever,
> I want to be dead
> forever and ever.[1]

And there's enough of the old Adam in us to respond positively in part at least to what Shaw has Adam say in one of his plays, "If only I can be relieved of having to endure myself forever! If only the care of this terrible garden may pass on to some other gardener—if only the rest and sleep that enable me to bear it from day to day, could grow after many days into an eternal rest, and eternal sleep, then I could face my days, however long they may last. Only, there must be some end, some end! I am not strong enough to bear eternity." Nor you! Nor I! At least if that is what Resurrection

[1] Quoted in J. Wallace Hamilton, *Who Goes There* (Westwood, N. J.: Fleming H. Revell, 1958), p. 15.

means. But that is what precisely it does not mean according to the Christian faith.

Resurrection is made easier for us to believe by the fact that all of us at times are aware that there is something eternal about life. You will recall Thornton Wilder in his play *Our Town* spoke to this. He has the stage manager say, "I don't care what they say with their mouths—everybody knows that *something* is eternal. And it ain't names and it ain't earth, and it ain't even stars—everybody knows in their bones that something is eternal, and that something has to do with human beings. All the greatest people ever lived have been telling us that for five thousand years, and yet you'd be surprised how people are always losing hold of it. There's something way down deep that's eternal about every human being."

The Christian faith is founded on the proposition that God has given us the answer to this responsive feeling of eternality in human life. It came in Jesus Christ. And it came on the day we mark as Easter Day. We are called to live under this decisive event. And what it did for the early disciples it can do for us. It can give us new courage and replace cowardice with valor. It can give us a new outlook on life and death, replacing our small focus on life with a wider vista of God's world. It can bring us new love which turns our self-seeking to self-giving. It can bring us new life which grows out of a new commitment to the Resurrection faith. It can be a here-and-now experience when we are raised above the fear of death, above prejudice and meanness, above selfishness into life in the spirit of Christ. Then we can share actively in

172

the redemption of our time. The key to it all is for us to hear and accept the promise of God in Jesus Christ who said, "I am the resurrection and the life, whoever believes in me will live, even though he dies, and whoever lives and believes in me will never die."